Where Science Meets Spirit:

The Formula for Miracles

By Brent Phillips

ISBN: 978-0-9802394-0-9

This book is dedicated to the loving memory of my father, Robert Lee Phillips, 1940-2007.

Table of Contents

Introduction: How an MIT-Trained Engineer Experienced a Miracle

As an engineer, scientist, skeptic, and generally practical person, I never expected to see even one miracle in my lifetime, let alone dozens or hundreds. Not only have I witnessed miracles myself, however, I even discovered how to make them! And now I teach a technique to show people a straight-forward, easy to learn process to create miracles in their own lives.

Of course, as a rational, discerning person I would encourage you to be highly skeptical of anyone who makes the claim that they have found a "Formula for Miracles". But at the same time, is it reasonable to close your mind to the possibility without first seeing for yourself whether or not this claim can be backed up? The *Formula for Miracles*™ described in this book is so real and so reliable, I am confident that if you try it out for yourself, you will see amazing results in your life.

But since a message is only as reliable as its source, before we get into the details of the *Formula for Miracles*™ it is important to understand where I came from and why I believe what I do. Certainly, I never had any idea that I would end up focusing my life's work on healing and mysticism! Like most people, I used to hold the notion that healing and miracles were not compatible with rigorous, practical, scientific thinking. Yet my journey has shown me that exactly the opposite is true: miracles are real and there is a practical, scientific way to draw them into your life!

I grew up as a fairly typical middle-class American kid and inherited the spiritual worldview dominant at the time: that we live in the cold, cruel world of insufficiency and competition, where we have to struggle and fight against forces out there in the world to ensure our survival and comfort. Like most of my peers, my future was planned out for me: grow up, go to college, get a job, and then spend the rest of my life devoting the vast majority of my time and energy to a career I did not really enjoy but that paid the bills. Magic and miracles were to be found only in books and movies, or thousands of years in the past. They certainly didn't seem to have any place in my 'normal' life. I couldn't have guessed that I would later find the link between computer software and miraculous instant healings.

Like many kids, I had a passion for computers and video games, and I can still remember the first time that I played a computer game. It was the late 1970s, and my friend's father was a professor at a local university, so he had a computer terminal at home that dialed into the mainframe on campus. Because the computer was a limited resource and games were given the lowest priority, we had to wait until the load on the system was low enough that we could log into the game. I remember eagerly rushing over to my friend's house in the afternoon after school, and waiting until enough computing resources were free so that we could play games on the mainframe. We played the classic game *Adventure* as often as we could, and I was hooked! Of course, at the time I had no idea how important my experience with computer games would be to later decoding the *Formula for Miracles* and instant healing.

Because programming computers seemed to be the one thing that I was genuinely interested in that I could also make a living at, it was an obvious focus for me. I taught myself how to program and spent a lot of time building and fixing computers and writing my own games. (I think I may be the only boy who ever asked for an assembly language reference book for his 13th birthday.) After high school I enrolled at MIT and majored in computer science, where I thrived in the intensely competitive environment.

Shortly after arriving at MIT in 1989 I discovered something truly incredible: the Internet! I had heard of the Internet only once before arriving at college, when the first major Internet worm made the news. As a forward-leaning research institution, MIT and sponsors from the computer industry had invested huge sums in what was called Project Athena, with the goal of making high-powered computer workstations with high-speed Internet connections available to all MIT students. Hence, the campus was dotted with clusters of Internet-enabled workstations that were free to use, though you sometimes had to wait a long time to get on a machine, especially the night before a major project was due.

When I was at MIT, I remember being afraid that after I left school I would lose access to the Internet. Widespread Internet access was still several years in the future; in fact, an MIT alum that I practiced martial arts with used to trade free software consulting to a local company in exchange for dial-up Internet access. Of course, in those days we had no idea what the future of the Internet would be, as at the time it was just an information sharing network for the government, universities, and companies doing advanced research.

Despite the primitive state of the Internet, I was absolutely fascinated by the online world, and I spent many late nights in chat rooms and on bulletin boards. At the time, I did not see the

Internet as a serious commercial opportunity, and I expected that I would graduate from college and get a "normal" software job and that the Internet and online world would remain just a hobby.

After four grueling years as an engineering major, I graduated at the top of my class (Phi Beta Kappa) and received multiple letters of commendation for exceptional academic performance from my professors. I then continued on to graduate school where I joined the Telemedia, Networks, and Systems group at the MIT Laboratory for Computer Science. There I performed my graduate research on sending audio and video over the Internet. To the best of my knowledge, my research group was the first ever to send live audio and video over the World Wide Web in 1994.

My stay in graduate school was truncated by the commercialization and then sudden popularization of the Internet in the mid 1990s. I had received my master's degree from MIT and qualified for and begun the PhD program in 1995 when, like many of my lab mates, I dropped out of school to pursue my fortune by moving to California to form an Internet company. I had two partners, one of them my long-time best friend. At the time they were both doing local computer repairs – replacing hard drives, installing anti-virus software and that sort of thing – and after many excited conversations I convinced them to start an Internet company. The Internet boom was the gold rush of my generation, and I was not going to miss out on it!

We formed a Web site development company, and before long we had a staff of over a dozen people and were developing high-profile Web sites for a number of Fortune 500 companies. While making Web sites was a good business, all three of us really wanted to be video game developers, so we formed another company devoted to making video games.

Because I was such a workaholic and so intensely devoted to building these companies, I was working 100+ hours a week on a regular basis. When you factor in that I typed over 100 words a minute and worked intensely, rarely taking breaks, you can understand that a huge strain was being put on my body. In retrospect, it is no surprise that it only took about a year before I was afflicted with devastating repetitive stress injuries.

For those who may think that computer injuries and other forms of repetitive stress are a joke, let me tell you that anyone who has experienced serious repetitive stress injuries knows that they are about as funny as being hit by a Mack truck (that is, not funny at all.) I suffered from terrible pain and restricted movement in my back, neck, and right arm and shoulder, and I was left unable to work or do much of anything. It was painful to shave myself, and it was painful to drive. Sometimes I had to ask other people to cut my food for me because it was too painful to do it myself. I could not even read books because it was too much strain on my arms and hands to hold a book open for more than a few minutes at a time. I was also losing sleep, because I would frequently wake up in the middle of the night in so much pain that I could not fall back asleep.

I was diagnosed with severe tendonitis across my entire upper body, along with several other diagnoses ending in "itis" (which is just a Latin term meaning something that is swollen or inflamed), as well as carpal tunnel syndrome and thoracic outlet syndrome. In fact, I had so many diagnoses of various versions of "itis" and "syndrome" that I used to joke that I had a severe case of "itis syndrome."

At first, I pursued the usual conventional remedies. I spent a lot of time with doctors and physical therapists, going through all manner of physical and occupational therapy and taking a whole array of drugs to try to manage the pain and inflammation. I did my homework and researched the very best doctors and therapists who worked in the field. I believed that if I could find the most respected and well-trained doctors, then surely they would be able to fix my problems so I could return to my life and make my millions on the Internet boom.

The fact that you are reading this book indicates that it did not work out that way. After a few years of splitting my time between the office and physical therapy, my condition only continued to worsen. Because I was so devoted to the Web site and video game companies I had founded, I trained myself to type one-handed so I could continue working. At one point I could actually type at 30 words per minute using only my left hand! In retrospect, this was incredibly stupid, because in a short time I was just creating the same problems in my left arm.

Eventually my inability to work a full time schedule caught up with me. Soon I found myself unable to work and in a legal dispute with my partners over the companies I had crippled myself to build. I was in near-constant pain, and doctors told me that I would never again be able to work full time with computers. The doctors told me that my condition was hopeless; in their lingo, I was "permanent and stationary," which meant that I was never going to get better.

At first I accepted this diagnosis and became extremely depressed. There was no way I could work at any sort of real job when a task as simple as dialing a phone caused me pain, so I ended up on disability. At the time I had no idea how I would be able to support myself for the rest of my life, let alone do something about the pain and physical limitations. If you think it might be fun to receive disability payments without needing to work, think again. It was an absolute nightmare for me, because not only could I not work, I also couldn't do anything else I enjoyed. I couldn't play computer games. I couldn't exercise. I couldn't Web surf, hold a phone, wash my car or clean my place. It is difficult to put into words the overwhelming frustration and despair I felt. And I was spending the equivalent of a full-time work week shuttling between various doctors and therapists, undergoing treatments that were sometimes terribly painful and always ineffective.

It was truly surreal how far I had fallen, and how fast. Just a few years before, I was one of the world's leading computer networking experts in the midst of the Internet boom, with the world at my feet and infinite possibilities. Somehow I had lost everything, was living in terrible pain and being told by doctors that I had no hope of recovering any semblance of a normal life.

Then, in 1999, I was introduced to the world of alternative medicine, and I hoped it would be my salvation. I got heavily involved with many forms of bodywork, homeopathy, osteopathy, chiropractors, Chinese doctors, energy healers, and all sorts of other stuff. I was spending all of my time and money experimenting with these treatments, still believing that it would be possible to fix my body and return to my previous life.

And this was not just a naïve hope; I had actually seen some amazing results from the practitioners I was working with, but not for my most serious problems. For example, when I first saw a homeopathic doctor, I had been having a problem with a persistent rash for a couple of years, and was spending a lot of money on prescription rash cream. He gave me a homeopathic remedy, and in less than three weeks the rash was gone, never to return.

Another time, I sprained my ankle and it hurt to put even a little bit of weight on my foot. But, after a single adjustment from my osteopathic doctor, I woke up the next morning and found my ankle was completely fine. There was no pain or tightness at all! So, I knew the people I was seeing were good, and I got some pretty incredible results on peripheral health problems, but nothing worked on my most serious afflictions: pain and movement restrictions in my hands, arms, shoulder, neck, and back.

This motivated me to find a lawyer and get my worker's compensation case reopened so I could continue to seek treatment. For the next seven years I lived on a combination of my savings, debt, and disability payments, and spent all my time, money, and energy in alternative treatments of various sorts. I estimate that during my odyssey I spent over $100,000 of my own money on various alternative health modalities, in addition to the conventional care I got through the state disability program. In addition to the orthopedic doctors, physical therapists, and occupational therapists, I went to numerous Chinese doctors, osteopaths, chiropractors, homeopaths, nutritional specialists, psychologists, psychiatrists, yoga classes, chi gong classes, pain specialists, naturopaths, energy healers (including Pranic healers and Reiki healers), Ayurvedic doctors, herbologists, movement re-trainers, and others. On top of this, I had something on the order of 1,000 hours of various kinds of deep tissue massage and bodywork done on me (that averages out to about 2 hours a week for 10 years.) At the same time, I took all sorts of supplements, suffered through many painful prolotherapy injections, did many kinds of body cleanses, and even tried different nutritional programs including a raw food diet.

Although a few of these treatments provided some marginal benefits for me, nothing was able to address or improve the core problems: tendinitis, bursitis, carpal tunnel syndrome, thoracic outlet syndrome, fibromyalgia, and a whole bunch of other Latin words that meant only that I was in pain and could hardly move and nobody knew what was really wrong with me or what to do about it.

In 2002 I had been in various treatments for several years without showing any significant improvement. I was scared to death of ending up homeless if I lost my disability benefits and wasn't able to work, so I agreed to have surgery done on my elbow. I had an overwhelmingly negative feeling about the surgery, but I didn't pay much attention to it because at the time I was a hardcore rationalist who thought that intuition was only for new-age hippy types.

As you may have guessed, the surgery was a disaster and the beginning of the worst chapter in my life. After the operation, my right arm was completely frozen at the elbow; I couldn't use it at all. Not only did this prevent me from common daily activities (for example, I could not floss my teeth,) but the frozen elbow also caused a variety of cascading problems through my neck and back. I endured a variety of awful treatments over the next four months in an attempt to free up my arm, including wearing devices called DynaSplints that put pressure on a frozen joint while you sleep. I even had a physical manipulation done under local anesthetic, which my surgeon later told me was a bad idea because sometimes people will have a heart attack from the intense pain.

I then agreed to undergo a second operation. This time, it actually did make progress in freeing up my arm, and I could move my arm more easily, although it was still far from functional. It would frequently freeze whenever I tried to use it, and it lacked a significant range of motion. Worst of all, I was spending several hours every day in a modern-day torture device called a CPM machine, which is a hydraulic monster that forcefully extends and bends your arm for you.

It was at this stage that my Aunt Lauren told me about a something that changed the course of my life. Her friend Terry O'Connell had experienced her own health crisis and found an alternative healing technique called Theta Healing. It not only significantly helped her, but she was so impressed by Theta Healing that she gave up her successful career in finance to pursue a new career as a full-time practitioner.

It seemed kind of crazy at first, but having tried everything else, I figured I had nothing to lose. So I made an appointment to try it out.

When I arrived for my session, Terry began telling me how Theta Healing works by using muscle testing to determine what beliefs are in the subconscious mind, and then using focused prayer techniques from a theta brainwave to reprogram the subconscious mind. The theory is that because the subconscious mind creates all aspects of our reality – including our health – reprogramming the portions of the subconscious mind creating an illness or disease will allow instantaneous healing.

It was amazing how well the Universe had prepared me for this situation. The two books that I had read prior to doing Theta Healing were *The New Revelations* by Neale Donald Walsh, which is about how our subconscious beliefs create and shape our reality, and *Power Versus Force* by David Hawkins, which is about how we can use muscle testing to query the subconscious mind. So I thought to myself, "Wow, this actually makes sense." However, I still was not convinced that Theta could do anything for me. I had endured a long string of esteemed and successful practitioners of various techniques, who had told me something like "Our treatment helps 99% of our clients to recover within 8 sessions." But guess who always fell into that 1% and who never saw any real improvement? (If you guessed me, you're correct!)

Terry and I talked about all sorts of things that were interesting, but did not seem directly connected to my health, including my parents, my relationship with God, various childhood experiences, my depression, and my career. We did a lot of muscle testing, and she used the Theta Healing technique to reprogram my subconscious belief systems. Then, after an hour or so of this, it was time for the physical healing. Terry mysteriously closed her eyes and went into some kind of trance. I closed my eyes and relaxed, and was surprised to feel a little popping or snapping occur in my elbow. Terry then said "Try your arm." Jaded and hardened by years of disappointment, I did not expect anything to happen, until I actually tried to use my arm.

It had worked – my arm had somehow been healed instantly!

I was able to bend and extend my arm smoothly without any pain or problems. My physical therapist and surgeon had told me that if I was lucky, getting to this point should have taken months of excruciatingly painful grinding and manipulations, if it could happen at all.

I was so relieved that I could use my arm again, all I could think was, *"Oh my God, it's a miracle!"* I remember thinking to myself, "I'm not exactly sure what this Theta Healing thing is, but I have got to learn it!"

Needless to say, this experience completely upended my understanding of reality and what is possible in life. Not only had I actually experienced an instant miracle healing, but I learned that this same Theta Healing process could be used to work with all the aspects of my life that I wanted to improve – health, finances, career, relationships, spiritual evolution – anything!

Despite my overwhelming initial enthusiasm, it was still a long and difficult journey to fully recover my health and build a new life for myself. Although my frozen elbow was honestly and truly healed, I had many other physical, emotional, and spiritual challenges that did not heal so miraculously. I had a lot more work to do before I could recover from the rest of my physical and psychological problems.

My introduction to Theta Healing was a profound turning point in my life. At the time I had been pursuing many different conventional and alternative therapies full-time for over seven years. Even though I knew I was seeing the best people and using the best techniques available, my health had continued to deteriorate even after the surgeries. But, with regular Theta Healing sessions, I was able to slowly and surely recover my health.

In particular, the same physical therapy, acupuncture, supplements, and bodywork that had done nothing for me for so long actually started to work! Little by little, I could see slow, measurable, and permanent improvement in my health. Within a few months I was able to drive, shave, cut my own food, and do a lot of little "life things" without the chronic pain I had lived with for so many years.

I immediately began doing everything I could to learn the Theta Healing technique myself. In addition to daily practice, I went to every Theta Healing seminar, practice group, and private session I could beg, borrow, or steal the money to attend. A year later, I felt confident enough to start doing it professionally. In 2004 I founded Theta Healing LA, with the purpose of sharing the incredible magic and power of Theta Healing with the world.

Just a few years ago I was suffering from "incurable" health problems, lived in terrible pain, poverty and loneliness, and had no hope of recovering a normal life. Today, I feel profoundly grateful that I have been able to use the Theta Healing technique to transform myself into a healthy, joyful, and prosperous person with amazing relationships and a phenomenal new career where I get to spend my days creating miracles in peoples' lives.

Not only have I been able to use the Theta Healing technique to change my own life, but it has also worked wonders for my clients and students. With my private session clients I have personally witnessed not just a handful, or even dozens, but literally hundreds of miracles. I've had clients who have reported instant miraculous healings from many different kinds of health problems, including such "difficult" or even "incurable" problems as cancer, asthma, allergies, broken bones, chronic lower back pain, and drug addiction. I've seen all manner of emotional traumas released and healed, allowing formerly angry, bitter, fearful, and traumatized people to truly live in joy and peace for the first time in their lives. I've seen relationships transformed, parents and children reconnecting, and marriages saved. And

I've helped many people who lived lives of struggle, sacrifice, debt, and poverty to begin to make money and experience financial abundance doing what they love. But don't take my word for it; experience it for yourself!

To emphasize that the miracles Theta Healing has worked in my life are not an isolated fluke, each chapter of this book begins with a short excerpt of a testimonial from one of my real-life Theta Healing clients, in their own words. The full text of each testimonial, as well as many other testimonials and free healing and spirituality resources, is available on my Web site at *www.Theta HealingLA.com.*

At the time of the printing of this book in 2008, the site contains over 70 real-life testimonials from normal people just like you who have experienced their own miracles from Theta Healing. In addition, there are hundreds of other people who got similar or better results but were not comfortable discussing the changes in their life with their full name and city disclosed in a public forum. I generally do not put up anonymous testimonials on the Web site, except in the case of socially stigmatized diseases such as HIV, because it's important to me that every testimonial is 100% genuine and can be easily verified. However, to protect my clients' privacy, in this book I have used only the initial of their last names, since unlike a Web site – which can be quickly edited at any time – after a book is printed it can't be changed or edited.

IMPORTANT DISCLAIMER: THIS IS NOT A MEDICAL TEXT

This book is intended for entertainment and informational purposes only. The author is not a licensed medical practitioner, and this book is neither intended to diagnose, treat, or cure any disease or condition, nor to be used as a medical reference, nor as a substitute for medical care from a licensed practitioner.

Chapter 1: Is There a Formula for Miracles?

"*Within 5 min my Dad was walking. WALKING without any assistance, fully dressed by himself!*"

Brent, I cannot express my gratitude and appreciation to you enough. My father had been extremely ill with emphysema, and has been bed-ridden and unable to walk. After your session with my Dad he "jumped" out of bed and expressed his desire to get out of the house for awhile. Well jumping out of bed is amazing in itself but he wanted to leave the house too! WOW! Today my Mom felt comfortable enough to go shopping with me and leave my Dad for a couple of hours. Poor Mom has not been out in weeks. She is too afraid of leaving my Dad. He needs her for everything. Well, when we got back he was laying in bed. When we asked how things were going he giggled. MY DAD GIGGLED. I cannot remember the last time the man laughed! He explained that he was just savoring each moment now that he has remembered how to breathe and was remembering how good it felt to feel good. He showed me how he is practicing his muscle testing and doing his homework. He is so happy. I do not remember the last time I saw my Dad happy.

He let us know that he was ready to get up which generally means 20 min of getting to the side of the bed going to the bathroom in a urinal than calling for Mom to dress him and wheel him to the sitting room. I was overwhelmed and moved to tears, within 5 min my Dad was walking...WALKING without any assistance, fully dressed by himself and announced he wanted to go Christmas shopping. He even got his own cup of coffee! My dad does not even like Christmas and has never, that I can remember gone Christmas shopping! Prior to the session with you he was on oxygen 24/7 and breathing treatments every 2 hours. Since the session he has not used his oxygen at all and has had 1/4 of a treatment yesterday with nothing today. Brent I am so grateful to you. All these things may sound silly to you to be so excited about but, to us it is a miracle. Thank you with all the love that I have.

SHERRI Y.
San Jose, California

Have we finally entered the era where science meets spirit? And is there really a *Formula for Miracles*? Fortunately, the answer is a resounding **yes** to both these questions. By bringing a rigorous and rational scientific analysis to the world of healing and spirituality, we can combine the best of both worlds to create "spiritual technologies" that facilitate healing and miracles in the same way that electronics technologies have facilitated computers and televisions.

As a scientist and engineer, it was at first extremely difficult for me to accept that an intuitive technique like Theta Healing was real and valid. However, over time I found that much of my understanding of scientific and engineering principles could be applied to the Theta Healing technique to explain how magic, miracles, and other mystical phenomena are not only possible, but easily accessible to everyone.

I found that Theta Healing was essentially a new form of *software engineering.* Instead of working in a medium of binary codes on computer systems, however, I was working in the medium of the human subconscious mind. And I found that, just as we can use engineering techniques to develop and debug software to create powerful computer programs, we can use these same techniques to develop and debug software in our subconscious mind to create powerful changes in our lives. Quite simply, if you do not like the "program" of your life written into the codes of your "subconscious software", you only need to change the software in your subconscious mind to see your life change. And the best part about it is that it does not require a person to be an engineer or even computer literate in order to make these changes!

By combining the worlds of science and spirit, it is possible to provide a clear, scientific explanation for phenomena such as instant healing, miracles, remote viewing, communication with the dead, and other 'mysteries'. Normal people – not just mystics and natural psychics – can learn how to do these things. Anyone can learn how to directly harness the full power of their subconscious mind to create miraculous instant healings, wealth, fulfilling relationships, and anything else they desire. This book aims to explain and demystify phenomena that have previously been seen as magical, mystical, or esoteric and show that indeed, there is a *Formula for Miracles*!

The Power of Human Consciousness

For a long time, people have wondered how consciousness arises out of the various physical structures in the body. It has been assumed more recently that human consciousness arises out of some proper combination of chemical and biological structures in the human brain, and many researchers have sought to isolate exactly where the physical seat of consciousness is. But nobody has ever been able to pin down exactly where or what this 'consciousness' really is.

Why? It turns out that there will never be an answer to these questions, because we have the whole process backwards. Instead of consciousness arising out of proper combinations of various types of matter, the truth is that matter arises from the proper combination of various types of consciousness! Physicists are now beginning to understand that matter and material reality are simply epiphenomena, or side effects, of our minds. In recent years, it has become clear to physicists working in cutting-edge research in cosmology and quantum physics that energy and consciousness are indeed the prime substrate of the Universe. That is, consciousness is the thing that makes up all physical matter. It is no coincidence, then, that many cutting-edge researchers in quantum physics (such as Michio Kaku and David Bohm) are becoming spiritualists!

This is such a powerful and important concept that it bears repeating. For the last few centuries we have believed that consciousness is created by combining the right sorts of chemical and biological structures, such as in the human brain. But it turns out that this understanding is incorrect. Instead, **all matter – the entire physical world – is actually created from consciousness!** While still not fully embraced by the mainstream scientific community, this understanding may be the single most important advance in science in the last hundred years.

This idea that matter is created from consciousness, and not vice-versa, is not just some new age, woo-woo concept. Instead, it is hard science and mathematics arising out of the equations of quantum physics and proven by decades of scientific experiments. The book *The Self Aware Universe* by physicist Amit Goswami provides an in-depth discussion of this theory.

Why does this matter for those of us who are not physicists? Simply put, if consciousness creates matter, then changing consciousness will change matter. Because our bodies are made out of matter, we often think that changing something in the body – say, a tumor – requires manipulating it directly on the physical level, such as with surgery or drugs. While this can work, it is also possible to change matter by changing the underlying consciousness that creates the matter.

There have been many documented examples of instantaneous healings where cancerous tumors have miraculously disappeared from the body. One example is the case of Vianna Stibal, the founder of Theta Healing, who in 1994 had a life-threatening cancer. Doctors had told her she had only a few months to live, and wanted to amputate her leg to buy her more time, when she experienced an instant healing. Despite the fact that she has the before and after MRI scans to provide it, many so-called rational people still dismiss her miraculous healing as a placebo effect.

How do these miraculous healings work? By changing the consciousness that creates the matter in the human body, it is possible to change the body, and instantaneous miracle healings are the result. This concept is as simple as it is profound: scientific theories conclude that consciousness and/or thought energy creates matter, so it makes sense that changing consciousness changes the matter it creates. So, yes, there truly is a rational scientific explanation for healings, miracles, and other seemingly inexplicable phenomena! Humans recognized that electricity and magnetism existed and worked in measurable yet mysterious ways long before we had the mathematical theories to explain and describe them. Similarly, the fact that science has so far been unable to explain miraculous instant healing with a high degree of mathematical certainty does not mean that there is no such explanation. Instead, it just means that we have not found the explanation. That is…until now. This book is an important step towards uniting science and spirit, and at the junction where science meets spirit we find the Formula for Miracles!

The Computer Metaphor for Understanding Healing and Miracles

In order to understand new concepts, it is oftentimes useful to explain things we do not understand in terms of things we do understand. Fortunately, we have the perfect metaphor available to demystify healing and miracles: the personal computer. By using the metaphor of the personal computer, it is possible to understand how we can all harness the ability to manipulate our consciousness and change both our physical bodies and our life experiences.

In this metaphor, human consciousness is like the software on a personal computer. We all know that the programs you see on the computer screen are created by the software running in the background. Hence, if you do not like what the programs are doing, you have to go and reprogram the software, or install new software. The computer hardware (the monitor, the printer, etc.) simply run the programs that are installed on the computer. If you have great software installed on your computer, you will have great programs, and your computer will be useful and fun. However, if you have the wrong software or buggy software on your computer, using the computer will be difficult and painful, and you will not be able to do very much with it, no matter how great your computer's hardware.

In our metaphor, the computer hardware is the world around us, including our bodies, and the computer software is our human consciousness. In the same way that the software you have installed on your computer determines what you can do with the computer, our consciousness – or "human software" –

determines our life experiences. So, if you do not like your health or some other part of your life experiences, you can identify and fix the "bugs" in the software of your consciousness to change your life. It's just that simple.

On a personal computer, reprogramming buggy software requires a programmer who has the proper training, experience, and tools to fix it. Similarly, to reprogram human consciousness, you need someone who has the proper training, experience, and tools to fix the software that is human consciousness. While it is not the only way to work with human consciousness, Theta Healing is an incredibly powerful, flexible, simple, and easy to learn method of reprogramming the software of human consciousness to change lives.

It is not necessary to have any advanced knowledge or experience with computers or software engineering in order to understand this process. If you have used a personal computer, you already know everything you need to understand this book and start creating miracles in your own life.

Having spent much of my life programming computers, I can say with certainty that it is about a zillion times easier to work with human consciousness by means of Theta Healing than it is to work with actual computer software. Writing computer software is generally difficult, time consuming, frustrating, and takes a high degree of training and experience to get it right. By contrast, working with human consciousness is something anyone can easily learn to do. If programming were like construction, then computer programming would be akin to building a skyscraper, which takes a great deal of time, money, planning, and expertise to get right. By contrast, changing human consciousness with Theta Healing is like building a porch, which anybody can do in a weekend with a bit of training and the proper tools.

We Can Learn How to Harness the Full Power of Our Minds

Many of us today have been exposed to the concept that we all create our own reality. It is our own human consciousness that directs and creates every life experience we have, in the same way that the software on a personal computer directs and creates every program that we run on the computer. Our spiritual teachers (including Jesus Christ and Buddha) have been trying to tell us this throughout history, and there are many wonderful books and movies that emphasize and illuminate this truth.

Truly, everything in our lives — including our health, our relationships, and our financial situation — is created by us. Just as a computer's software controls what that computer's hardware does, our consciousness is arranging and creating every experience we have. We are all the captains of our own ship and the creators of our own destiny!

On the other hand, none of us consciously chose the various problems in our lives. We do not remember signing up for health crises, pain, divorce, abuse, emotional traumas, poverty, depression, violence, meaningless jobs, or any of the other difficulties we experience in our lives. So, how is it that — if we are really creating and in control of every aspect of our lives — we do not remember creating the problems and tragedies that so many of us experience?

The answer is that we do not create our lives with our conscious minds, but instead, we do it with our subconscious minds. Our consciousness includes both, but it is the subconscious mind that does most of the "heavy lifting" in shaping and creating all the experiences in our lives, both good and bad.

The subconscious mind can be understood as software that creates your life experiences, in the same way that software on a computer creates the programs that you run on it. Because most of us do not understand what is in our subconscious mind or how it works, it seems to us that we are helpless victims living in a cold, cruel world where external powers (other people, the weather, governments, big companies, etc.) control us. Hence, it seems that bad things – illness, injury, tragedy, and so on – 'just happen', because we do not understand or remember how we created these experiences. So, we blame factors outside of ourselves for our life problems, and we think that changing these external factors (mostly other people!) is the only way that we can fix our problems and change our lives.

However, the real truth is that, no matter what happens in your life, it is all being created for you, by you, according to your own consciousness. And this consciousness can be understood as the software of your subconscious mind. This is a powerful concept. **Because you are the creator and source of all the problems in your life, you hold within you all the power needed to solve these problems**. However, it will not happen automatically; first you need to learn how to access and apply this power, which will be explained in this book. If you are using a computer program and it has a bug in it, then fixing the bug in the program's software will cause the program to start functioning more to our liking. In a sense, fixing a computer bug is a form of instant healing. Similarly, if you can identify and change the consciousness inside yourself that is causing some problem in your life, the problem will disappear, sometimes instantly. It does not matter if it is a health problem, a financial challenge, or even a difficult relationship; all of these things are created out of our consciousness, and changing our consciousness will create different experiences. Illnesses heal, relationships become whole and fulfilling, and financial prosperity results – all from changing the underlying consciousness.

The best part is that anybody can learn to do this! I was never a natural psychic, and I had no interest in becoming an intuitive until I experienced the miracle that healed my arm. Despite the fact that I was a hard-core engineer, scientist, and agnostic, I was able to quickly and easily learn and use the Theta Healing technique to "debug" human consciousness and change lives.

The Truth about the Law of Attraction

Since the Law of Attraction was featured on Oprah, it has received a lot of press, and spawned an entire industry of Law of Attraction coaches, seminars, books, videos, and other Law of Attraction tools. The Law of Attraction states that *like attracts like*. The theory is that if you shift your thinking and attitude to be more positive, then you will start attracting more positive things into your life.

If the hype around the Law of Attraction is to be believed, then by just shifting your thinking, you should be able to be completely healthy, make a million dollars, and find your soul-mate, all by the end of the month! And while a few people have watched a DVD or read a book or attended a positive thinking seminar and been able to heal from cancer, or make a ton of money, the vast majority of us see little or no major shift in our lives and just get frustrated. This is because 'shifting your thinking' only involves your conscious mind, which contains at most 10-20% of your manifesting power. The other 80-90% is held in the mysterious subconscious mind. And guess what happens if 10% of your mind wants one thing and 90% of your mind wants something else? You got it: the 90% will win every time! And that is why the Law of Attraction does not work for many people; they make their vision boards and say their affirmations, yet do not see their lives improve.

However, if you are able to fully involve 100% of your mind – conscious and subconscious – then the Law of Attraction really does work, and you really can heal instantly, make a million dollars, and live a life filled with loving, fulfilling relationships.

Practical Miracles for Everyday Use

I am a practical person, and there is only one reason why I have devoted myself to the study and practice of Theta Healing and working with the subconscious mind: *because it works*. Of course, it does not always work in the way that we would like, or on the timetable we would like. If I find some other technique or way of understanding things that works better to change my life, I will happily learn it as well. However, this has not happened yet, and in my opinion Theta Healing is – by a considerable margin – the most powerful and effective technique for personal transformation available to us today. I continue to use Theta Healing because it continues to deliver practical and consistent results!

I have used Theta Healing in various experiments on my life and on a variety of issues – health, money, relationships, and others – and have consistently found that it makes a noticeable and measurable difference. And it doesn't just work... it works really, really well!

Unfortunately, too many of the great books and articles available on spirituality, healing, and metaphysics are full of wonderful high-minded ideals and concepts, but provide little or no practical tools to apply to our day-to-day lives. I know that I was introduced to some truly profound and life changing concepts and materials when I was in the middle of my years of pain and disability. However, these great concepts of "we are all one" and "love is all there is" and "we all have the power within us to heal instantly" were nice warm, fuzzy thoughts to have sitting at home on a Saturday evening, but did nothing on a practical level to help me cope with the problems in my regular daily life.

This book is just the opposite. It is intended to be primarily a source of practical information so that you may understand how to harness the power of your subconscious mind for healing, manifestation, and whatever other forms of miracles you wish to create. If there is something about your life that you would like to change, you can identify what is really happening – finding the "core" of the problem – and then take steps to effect a meaningful and permanent resolution to the situation by changing the underlying consciousness creating the problem.

No matter how difficult, terrible, painful or impossible our circumstances, we can take comfort in knowing that we have created every aspect of our reality subconsciously. And this understanding gives us the exact tools and power we need to change things. Why? Because if you created it, you can fix it!

Chapter 2: What the Bleep is a Theta?

"The damage from the accident is healed, and it happened in seconds."

My name is George, and I got a concussion in a high speed car accident 5 month ago. I was slowly getting better, but then I started having migraines and they lasted three weeks in a row. I was so frustrated that I was getting worse and had to deal with all that suffering. My therapist and life coach suggested that I went to a conference by Brent. Usually I do not go to those "new age" things, but then I found out that Brent was an engineer before becoming a healer. Being an engineer myself I thought that could be interesting.

I was selected for the demonstration, and in minutes he found out that the pain from the accident and the awful past life thing were all related. He did his healing. Before that, I was alleviating the pain from the migraines by reducing the blood pressure going to my brain, sometimes to the point of numbness, and by avoiding strong emotions.

Right after the healing my emotions were high, very high, and the blood pressure going to the brain was high too because of the excitement, and I had no migraine whatsoever, they were totally gone and never came back. In the following days I tested my limits by doing some physical exercise (could not do anything since the accident) and some yoga postures where I could briefly have my head down (like the downward facing dog) I found out there is no portion of my brain to feel sore, the damage from the accident is completed healed, and it happened in seconds.

Today I had another healing session with Brent to work on my eyesight. Since the accident, trying to focus my vision would quickly give me a headache, especially while using a computer, so I was using reading glasses for all those tasks. The amazing thing right now is that I just wrote this testimonial looking at the screen with my bare eyes, and I feel fine!

GEORGE M.
Santa Monica, California

In order to work with human consciousness, we first need a way to measure it. This can be done by measuring brainwaves. Brainwaves are the electric and magnetic fields that our brains produce. Different brainwaves are associated with different states of consciousness. Therefore, by exploring and measuring brainwaves, we can gain insight into what is going on inside the human mind.

Theta Healing is named after and uses the theta brainwave. So what exactly is a brainwave?

The human brain is a complicated electrical and chemical mechanism. As it operates, it creates electrical and magnetic fields in and around the brain and head. By attaching electrodes to the scalp and using a device known as an electroencephalogram (EEG), we can view and analyze the traces of electrical activity in the brain that represent the brainwaves.

Like all waves, brainwaves have a frequency, measured in cycles per second or Hertz (abbreviated Hz), which is the number of cycles a wave goes through in one second. So, a lower Hertz number represents a slower wave, and a higher Hertz number represents a faster wave.

Brainwaves are categorized by their frequency. There are five kinds of brainwaves: alpha, beta, theta, delta, and gamma, but the brainwave we are most interested in is the theta brainwave.

Theta brainwaves are very slow brainwaves, at four to seven Hz (or cycles per second.) Why is this particular brainwave so important? It is because the theta brainwave is the amazing key that unlocks the full power of our minds. It allows us to do things that were previously relegated to the realm of mystics, such as miraculous instant healings.

The reason that the theta brainwave is so powerful is that we can use it to directly access and even reprogram the subconscious mind. The most common way we naturally achieve a theta brainwave state is when we are sleeping and dreaming, during what is known as "rapid eye movement" or REM sleep. In short, theta is the brainwave of dreaming. (Besides dreaming, another time we naturally go into theta is when we are playing video games. Video games literally hypnotize us, and this is why some people – particular children and teenagers – can play video games for hours yet it seems like only a few minutes have passed.)

Dreaming has been closely linked to psychic ability and prophecy since the beginning of time. Even when I was young, and thought that all psychics were phonies and that miracles only happened thousands of years in the past, I always had a strong intuition that there was incredible inherent power in our dreams.

By achieving a conscious theta brainwave – that is, by achieving the brainwave of dreaming sleep while we are awake – it is possible to gain conscious and direct access to the subconscious mind. This in turn allows us to identify and fix the defective programs in your subconscious mind that is resulting in injury, illness, poverty, or any other aspect of your life that you wish to change. This makes sense intuitively, because when we are dreaming, it is our subconscious mind that is running the show. Hence, if we can access the dreaming brainwave while we are awake and conscious, we can work consciously with the normally mysterious, invisible, and off-limits subconscious mind! The theta brainwave is the master key that allows us to directly access the subconscious mind, and the Theta Healing technique makes this key available to us.

History is filled with examples of those who have used the theta brainwave without fully understanding exactly what it is they were doing. One good example is Edgar Casey, known as "The Sleeping Prophet", who was able to achieve the theta brainwave in a semi-awake, semi-asleep state and use it for channeling, healing, and prophecies.

However, through most of history, we did not have the science or technology to measure or understand mystical states and experiences. People did not understand *how* psychic phenomena occurred, but only observed that they did. In the same way that primitive people used the idea of spirits and gods to explain the natural world, various theories of psychic phenomena have appeared and reappeared throughout history in the stories told in various mythologies, religions, and the occult or "mysteries".

As modern understandings of anatomy and cellular biology have rendered many old theories of medicine and health obsolete and made possible many new amazing technologies and procedures, modern understandings of the brain and its structure and functions also serve as the underpinnings for comprehending mystical and psychic phenomena. Human beings truly are wired into a universal Web of energetic connections and consciousness. And what is the gateway between the energetic world and the physical world? It is our own human bodies and minds, and in particular, the theta brainwave!

Scientists and spiritualists alike now agree that working with the subconscious mind has tremendous potential to deeply and profoundly affect both ourselves and the environment around us. Unfortunately, the society in which we live has not fully understood the means by which we can access and use the power of our subconscious. There have been innumerable different techniques for measuring and reprogramming the subconscious (albeit nearly all of them indirect), which have enjoyed varying degrees of success. Visualizations, speaking mantras, hypnotism, and prayers are all time-tested (though often ineffective) techniques of working with the subconscious mind. Sometimes these techniques work, and sometimes they do not, and until recently nobody really understood why. Fortunately, with the advent of the Theta Healing technique and modern understandings of physics and technology, it is finally possible to explain and demystify miraculous healings and psychic phenomena, and turn them into practical tools for improving our day-to-day lives!

What is Theta Healing?

Theta Healing is a technique of achieving a conscious theta brainwave and using it to directly access the subconscious mind. This allows us to identify and transform the subconsciously held beliefs, attitudes, expectations, and traumas that we have brought into our lives via the Law of Attraction (the principle that like attracts like.) In short, it is the tool we use to reprogram the software of human consciousness.

Our subconscious mind literally manifests and creates every aspect of our reality, from our health and surroundings to our experiences and the way in which we interact with other people . Hence, with a technique to quickly and effectively reprogram the internal software of the subconscious mind, we can transform ourselves and truly change our lives.

If you doubt that we are the makers of our own reality, there are a few different ways you can mollify your skepticism. First, our great spiritual teachers have all been telling us the same thing for thousands of years: that we are able to create and manifest anything with the power of our minds. (For example, Jesus said "If you faith as big as a mustard seed you can move mountains.", and "These things, and more, you shall do.") Unfortunately, these teachers usually did not give us a reliable, clear, and simple step-by-step process to do so.

Second, and more importantly, the proof is in the pudding! In other words, the results of the Theta Healing process speak for themselves. I encourage you to always be skeptical; do not believe anything you read here just because I said so – but instead, try the techniques and see for yourself that they work! If you are able to access and reprogram the defective programs in your subconscious, you will see your life change as a result. It does not matter if you do not believe in God or theta brainwaves or any of the explanations presented in this book or elsewhere. I like to say that *Just because you do not believe in gravity, does not mean you can fly....and just because you do not believe in airplanes does not mean that you cannot!* In other words, gravity affects us, and airplanes defy gravity and let us fly, no matter what ideas we have about them. The power of the subconscious mind and Theta Healing work in exactly the same way: even if you do not believe in them, you can experience that they are real and effective through the results they create. I did not believe in healing or miracles either. However, without knowing whether or not Theta Healing would help me, I was still open and humble enough to make the appointment where I experienced my frozen arm miraculously heal in an instant!

Though it is an intuitive process and a form of energy healing, Theta Healing can also be understood as an engineering discipline. The process by which it operates is a form of spiritual or consciousness technology, where engineering is done upon human consciousness instead of on computer software. Much as anybody with the inclination and interest can learn to program a computer, anybody with the inclination and interest can learn to reprogram the subconscious mind for healing, wealth, love, and whatever else your heart desires. Fortunately, you do not need to know how to program computers in order to derive great benefits from using them, and likewise you can use the technique of Theta Healing to experience wonderful changes in your life without knowing exactly how the process works.

The Genesis of Theta Healing

The Theta Healing technique (at least in its modern incarnation) was developed by accident in 1994 by Vianna Stibal. As with many people, Vianna got involved with alternative health because she had no choice. She had developed a life-threatening cancer, and was given a death sentence by her doctors. She refused to give up, and did everything she could to heal her cancer naturally. Because she felt the cancer was caused by toxicity (specifically mercury), she did a variety of cleanses and diets, and was spending four hours a day in a special infrared sauna to detoxify her body. She even got herself certified as a Naturopath in her quest to heal herself.

She was so sick from the cancer that she could not hold a regular full-time job. Being a single mother who was supporting three children, she started doing psychic readings and massage work to make ends meet and put food on the table for her family. Vianna had been a natural psychic her whole life. She experienced a lot of success giving people psychic readings, even though she did not really understand what she was doing or why it worked.

Then, one day, Vianna was at a party where one of the guests was complaining of a pain in her stomach. Vianna did a psychic reading on the cause of the pain, and while she was doing the reading she decided to tell the pain to go away so that this person would stop complaining about it. Surprisingly, it worked, and the pain disappeared!

After experiencing similar success healing somebody else, Vianna decided to try the same technique on her own cancer. She commanded that her leg be healed, and the cancer miraculously disappeared, along with all the pain and illness! Her cancer had been completely and instantly healed.

Understandably, Vianna was transformed by this experience. Word spread of her miraculous healing, and soon people were coming from all around the world to be healed by this woman from Idaho. However, as Vianna worked with more and more people, she found that while some people did in fact heal instantly, many other people did not, and she did not understand why. She then spent the next several years of her life exploring, expanding and refining the healing technique. Along the way, she developed not only a clear understanding of how and why some healings worked and others did not, but also a teachable framework that could be communicated in a linear fashion to "normal" people who were not mystics or natural psychics.

Chapter 3: Brainwaves

"I had received an instantaneous, miracle healing from Brent!"

I went to a Quantum QXCI/SCIO practitioner because I wanted to know whether or not a cracked tooth was causing a larger problem throughout my body. The answer for that question was a negative, but I was shocked with the result that liver cancer was showing up as a "red alert." Then I remembered that for two to three months I had been experiencing dull pains, sometimes escalating to sharp pains, in my right side and thinking this was a strange place to hurt for indigestion or an ulcer. My immediate thought was to make an appointment with Brent. We did our session via the phone on a Sunday morning. Test results from the allopathic doctor also showed no liver problems at all. As further proof, all pains have disappeared. I had received an instantaneous, miracle healing from Brent!

However, since the original practitioner was not a doctor, I decided to go to a doctor and a nationwide trainer for the QXCI/SCIO just to see if there was anything else going on in my body. He confirmed that I did not have liver cancer, but this time I was told that I was carrying a breast cancer miasm (or genetic propensity) in my energy field. This made sense since my grandmother had died of breast cancer. This second time Brent worked on me for breast cancer and cancer generally.

When I returned for a check-up, the computer programs indicated that I am completely clear of all cancer and cancer miasms. What a small price and such a short time (less than one session each) for the priceless gift of eliminating potential life threatening diseases in my energy field. As a friend said to me, there was never any doubt in your mind that you would eliminate these instantaneously with Theta Healing. Brent is a brilliant Theta Healing practitioner and instructor.

NAOMI M.
Fullerton, California

Healing and Theta Brainwaves

Vianna came to understand that the key to the success of her healing and psychic reading technique was her ability to access a conscious theta brainwave. However, when she told other people this theory, they told her that she must be wrong, because they believed it was impossible to achieve a conscious theta brainwave without being a master guru who meditated full-time for at least 30 years. She was told that she would have to start by meditating to achieve an alpha brainwave, and that only after decades of dedicated practice could she hope to someday achieve a conscious theta brainwave.

Vianna did not accept that it was so difficult to get to a theta brainwave, so she partnered with a scientist who built an EEG for her. When they hooked it up to her and she used her healing technique, it provided hard proof for her theory: the EEG showed that Vianna was actually achieving a waking and conscious theta brainwave when doing healings!

The Various Human Brainwaves

There are five different brainwave states, described below.

Beta brainwaves, measured at 13-40 Hz, are the brain state of our normal waking consciousness. Nearly all forms of action, thinking, and problem solving are done with a beta brainwave.

Most people spend the vast majority of their waking lives in a beta state.

Alpha brainwaves, measured at 7-13 Hz, are the brain state of relaxation and meditation. The alpha brainwave is associated with creativity and super learning, where the brain learns at a faster and deeper level than it does in beta. Many meditation and energy healing techniques cultivate and utilize an alpha brainwave for relaxation and healing.

Theta brainwaves, measured at 4-7 Hz, are the brain state of REM sleep (dreams), hypnosis, lucid dreaming, and the barely conscious state just before sleeping and just after waking. Theta is the border between the conscious and the subconscious world. By learning to use a conscious, waking theta brainwave, we can access and influence the powerful subconscious part of ourselves. While in the theta brainwave, the mind is capable of deep and profound learning, healing, and growth. It is the brainwave where our minds can connect to the Divine and manifest changes in the material world.

Delta brainwaves, measured at less than 4 Hz, are the brain state of deep sleep and unconsciousness.

Gamma brainwaves, measured at 22+ Hz, are the brainwaves of hyper-alertness, perception, and the integration of sensory input. When time seems to slow down during a car accident, the brain is entering a gamma brainwave; in fact, time is not slowing down so much as the brain is speeding up. When using the Theta Healing technique, the brain is actually using both the theta and gamma brainwaves.

Beta (14-30 Hz)

Concentration, arousal, alertness, cognition

Higher levels associated with Anxiety, disease, feelings of separation, fight or flight

Alpha (8 - 13.9 Hz)

Relaxation, superlearning, relaxed focus, light trance, increased serotonin production

Pre-sleep, pre-waking drowsiness, meditation, beginning of access to unconscious mind

Theta (4-7.9 Hz)

Dreaming sleep (REM sleep)
Increased production of catecholamines (vital for learning and memory), increased creativity

Integrative, emotional experiences, potential change in behavior, increased retention of learned material

Hypnagogic imagery, trance, deep meditation, access to unconscious mind

Delta (0.1-3.9 Hz)

Dreamless sleep
Human growth hormone released

Deep, trance-like, non-physical state, loss of body awareness

Access to unconscious and "collective uncon-scious" mind,

Four categories of brain wave patterns

There is a great deal of research activity currently underway to further explore the link between brain activity, physiology, and phenomena such as psychic healing. Combining the science of brainwaves with spirituality is already yielding interesting new products such as the various meditation CDs that use binaural beat technology to bring the listener's brain to a particular brainwave. If you have a meditation CD that specifies that you should listen to it through headphones, it is probably a binaural beat CD designed to help you achieve the slower brainwaves, particularly alpha and theta. (My own binaural beats meditation CD, designed with the help of one of my students, Jesse Stern, was made specifically to put the listener into a deep theta brainwave and is available at the *www.Theta Healingla.com* website.)

Decades of research on brain activity and consciousness have shown that our state of being and how we feel is directly connected to our brainwave activity. For example, people who are extremely awake and alert are probably in the beta brainwave, while people who experience a predominance of the delta brainwave are likely unconscious, and possibly in a coma!

Much research and anecdotal evidence have also shown that many paranormal and psychic phenomena are associated with the lower frequency brainwaves, and particularly the theta state.

A Common Misconception about Brainwaves

It is a common misconception that the brain has only one type of brainwave at a time. In fact, all of the brainwaves are active in the brain at all times, but at varying levels. So, the brain always has alpha waves, beta waves, theta waves, gamma waves, and delta waves *simultaneously*. What we really mean when we say that the brain is in a "theta brainwave" is that the theta brainwave is stronger (meaning it displays higher amplitude on an EEG) than the other brainwaves. In other words, it is the dominate brainwave at that given moment. *what dominat or longest*

For example, an EEG may read that a person's brain has alpha waves with amplitude of "3", beta waves with amplitude of "10", theta waves with amplitude of "2", delta waves with amplitude of "1", and gamma waves with amplitude of "1". This means that the brain is in the beta state. While in the beta state the other brainwaves are still present, but they are simply not as strong as the beta brainwaves.

To say that you are in a conscious theta brainwave does not mean that you do not have the alpha, beta, gamma or delta brainwaves. Instead, it simply means that the theta brainwaves are stronger (higher in amplitude) than any of the others.

For example, if an EEG is attached to my head and a brainwave scan is done when I am busy reading a book, you might find that the beta brainwaves (13-22 Hz) are stronger than any others (alpha, theta, delta, gamma). This makes sense, because when we are reading we are moving our brains into a beta state. If you later attached an EEG to my head when I was sleeping and dreaming, you would likely find that the theta brainwaves (4-7 Hz) were the strongest, because theta is the brainwave of dreaming sleep.

So, to achieve a conscious theta brainwave we are simultaneously reducing the amount of brainwave activity in the beta range and increasing the amount of brainwave activity in the theta range.

With a conscious theta brainwave, anyone can learn to perform a variety of "mystical" and "psychic" phenomena such as psychic body scans, future readings, guardian angel readings, remote viewing, and instant healings. This is possible because the conscious theta brainwave allows us to directly access and recode our subconscious minds. That is, we can use the theta brainwave to quickly and easily reprogram the subconscious software inside of ourselves to create a different reality (or new program).

Chapter 4: The Subconscious Mind and Muscle Testing

"I talked with Brent and could not believe the improvement in my neck..."

I had excessive pain in my neck from 2 herniated disks. My Fiancé came home and said she set this thing up with a healer, and asked if I would do it. I said I would even though I really did not believe in it. Well I talked with Brent and could not believe the improvement in my neck, the pain lessened to such an extent that I felt like myself again for the first time since my injury. If you are like me and the pains are always there, it is worth anything to have it released. Brent is the man for the job! Take it from a former non-believer who now believes. He is amazing!!!

SCOTT V.
Waterloo, New York

- -

The power of the subconscious mind has been acknowledged, though perhaps not well understood, for a long time. Many of our finest authors, teachers, and leaders have been trumpeting the power of the subconscious, claiming that if we only learn to harness the power of the subconscious, we can live the life of our dreams.

To better understand the subconscious mind, let us start by examining what we know about the conscious mind. We know that the physical seat of the conscious mind is in the frontal lobe of the brain, and that anything that interferes with this area of the body will impair the higher learning functions. For example, if you have a lobotomy, you will lose the higher thought functions because the part of the brain that is responsible for abstract thinking and higher thought functions has been removed.

But what exactly is the subconscious mind? And where is it in the body?

This is an excellent question, and it has a very simple answer: the subconscious mind is your entire body! If this seems surprising, think about the stories you may have heard about people who have received organ transplants, and then took on the memories or personality characteristics of the donor. The book *A Change of Heart* describes the experiences of Claire Silvia, who received a heart transplant and immediately thereafter experienced radical personality changes and shifts in her food preferences. She had always been calm and passive before the transplant, but became much more aggressive and demanding afterwards. Further, before the transplant, she was a dancer who preferred health foods, but after she had inexplicable cravings to eat deep fried chicken nuggets. And not only did it turn out that the man who had donated the heart to her was known to be aggressive and confrontational, but when he was found dead there were deep fried chicken nuggets in his jacket pocket!

These types of phenomena occur more frequently than you may think, and they could not happen if the mind were located entirely in the brain. In fact, every cell of our body has its own memory and experiences, and it is likely that some of the difficulty science has had narrowing down exactly how the brain processes and stores memories might be because this process does not occur only in the brain. There are numerous doctors and scientists who have developed intriguing theories of cellular memory, and there is much anecdotal evidence to support them. Lynette Taggart's book *The Field* provides an excellent overview of various scientific experiments that prove the existence of this sort of cellular memory.

If we think about many of the common experiences that we humans have and the phrases that we use to describe them, we find that we already know intuitively about the power of the body's cellular intelligence. For example, we talk about having a "gut feeling" that guides us and is connected to a higher intelligence. We talk about our "hearts bursting" when we are overcome with emotion. We say this because we know instinctively, though perhaps not cognitively, that our organs and our bodies have their own intelligence beyond that which is consciously available to us. Even the most hard-core atheists and agnostic skeptics recognize that "hunches" and "intuition" are a part of the human experience. Further, it is not necessary to invoke God or any supernatural being to explain how the larger part of our own personal intelligence – the body's intelligence – influences and guides us, although this process may not be as directly available to us as our conscious knowledge.

Our various financial gurus, entrepreneurs, and best-selling authors are all telling us that it is our subconscious mind that creates our reality, and that the most effective path to changing the world around us is to change what is inside ourselves. One good example is T. Harv Eker's book *Secrets of the Millionaire Mind,* where he discusses the concept of the *subconscious financial blueprint.* He discusses how it is not your background, education, knowledge or even who you know that matters in determining your financial prosperity: instead, the only thing that really matters is what is in your *subconscious financial blueprint.*

I agree wholeheartedly with this concept and believe that this is an excellent example to help us understand how to use the power of the subconscious to change ourselves and our lives. Much as the blueprint for a building determines what the building will look like, the subconscious financial blueprint for our lives determines how much money and material abundance we will experience.

However, the concept of the power of the subconscious mind is not limited only to finance and wealth. Indeed, you have a subconscious blueprint for every aspect of your life! You have a subconscious blueprint for your relationships, and changing this blueprint is the most permanent and effective way of transforming and improving these relationships. You have a subconscious blueprint for your health, and changing this blueprint is the most permanent and effective way of healing your body and your mind. You have a subconscious blueprint for your relationship with your neighbors, and one for the foods that you are allergic to, and for your parents. The list could go on forever. It is sometimes difficult to accurately describe the power and potential of being able to directly work with the subconscious mind because it is so critical to every aspect of our existence.

What is the "Veil" Between Life and Death?

In spiritual and esoteric literature, there is much discussion of the "veil" which separates the physical reality of the existence we understand from the "other side", or the energy realm of spirits and ancestors. People who have an affinity or ability to access the energetic realm are labeled natural psychics. For the most part we have not been able to understand why they are different or why they have the abilities they do. Instead, we just chalk it up to one more mystery of existence.

However, we can now examine these phenomena and begin to understand why certain people have these abilities and others do not. This "veil" is indeed real, and it is because of this veil that the majority of people in the modern world are not able to directly experience or access the energetic realm. As a result, many of them do not believe it exists at all. However, this "veil" is not some supernatural curtain, which only a chosen few with psychic gifts have the ability to see past. Instead, the veil is simply the accumulation of programs in our subconscious minds that tell us that it is impossible, difficult or dangerous to access, understand or use the energetic realm. Thus, it takes nothing more than clearing away the old burdens, traumas, and reactions held in our subconscious minds before we can "thin the veil" and begin to have our own experiences with the energetic realm. Instant healings, communication with the dead, talking to guardian angels, remote viewing, past life regressions, and more are not only possible but easy when your subconscious belief systems do not get in the way.

The Meaning of "Subconscious"

Before proceeding with our discussion of the subconscious mind, it is important to clarify exactly what this term means. In the context of this book, *subconscious* is used as a general term to encompass everything that is beyond the conscious mind. So, for our purposes, we do not differentiate between the unconscious mind and the subconscious mind.

By contrast, the Jungian school of psychology divides the mind into conscious, subconscious, and unconscious. Other schools of thought use additional terms to mean different parts of the mind beyond the conscious, subconscious, and unconscious. For example, Neale Donald Walsh uses the term super-conscious mind in the *Conversations with God* books to mean the soul's intelligence, or higher self, that guides our life decisions. But, for our purposes in this book, everything other than the conscious mind – including the unconscious, super-conscious, and any other term – are all included into the generic term "subconscious mind."

Muscle Testing

Once it is recognized that the subconscious mind is the most important factor in manifesting our health and circumstances, it is natural to ask "How do we know what is in the subconscious?"

It is easy to find out what is in somebody's conscious mind: you just ask them, and they will tell you the answer. However, things are not so straightforward with the subconscious mind. Fortunately, there is a technique known as *muscle testing* that can be used to give us the answers we seek.

Remember that the subconscious mind is in the entire body. Hence, if we could somehow ask the body questions, we could determine what is in the subconscious. And fortunately, we can do this quickly and easily with the technique of muscle testing.

How does muscle testing work? In short, when you say or think something that resonates as true with the subconscious mind, the electrical and magnetic fields around the body actually become stronger. Similarly, when you say or think something that resonates as false with the subconscious mind, the electrical and magnetic fields around the body become weaker. These electrical and magnetic fields around the body are very real, and can be measured with highly sensitive electrical equipment.

Because the strength of a muscle is influenced by the strength of the electromagnetic field which surrounds that muscle, we can measure muscle strength to determine the strength of the electromagnetic field around a person. How does this work? Anybody who has ever gone through rehabilitation after surgery or otherwise been in a physical therapist's office knows that they are full of electrical equipment. Why? Because muscles are really just electro-magnetic machines. The strength of a muscle's contraction is proportional to the strength of the electromagnetic field which surrounds it. So, muscles actually become stronger when they are in stronger fields, and weaker when they are in weaker fields.

Consequently, if a man named John says *"I am a man"* or *"My name is John"*, these statements resonate as true with his subconscious mind and his field, and as a result, his muscles become stronger. This is a very real, very physical effect that can be measured with sensitive electrical equipment! Conversely, if John states *"I am a woman"* or *"My name is Joan"*, these statements will resonate as false with his subconscious and his field. As a result, his muscles will go weak.

Because the strength of a muscle is related to the strength of the electromagnetic field in which the muscle resides, it is possible to indirectly measure the strength of a field by measuring the strength of the muscle. Specifically, if you measure the strength of a muscle when you are saying or thinking something that resonates true with the subconscious, you will actually measure that your muscles are stronger than when you are thinking or saying something that resonates false with the subconscious mind!

Have you ever watched guys lifting heavy weights at the gym? They are usually telling each other things like *"Yes!"* and *"Push it!"* and *"Work!"* and *"You can do it!"* Why? Because they know intuitively that positive statements and thoughts actually make the muscles stronger! If you doubt this, go to the gym and do an experiment. First, load up a gym machine with a heavy weight, and say *"Yes! Yes! Yes"* as you lift the weights, and see how many repetitions you can do. Then, rest for a few minutes, and repeat the process saying *"No! No! No!"* You will find that you can actually lift more weight making positive statements than negative statements.

Let us walk through this process step by step with an example. There are many methods of muscle testing, but the one that people are most familiar with is called the arm lever test. To do this test, the person being tested extends her arm out from her body at shoulder level and holds it strong so that it cannot be pushed down. If the person being tested has a strong field, the muscles will be strong, and the person doing the testing will not be able to push down the arm. However, if the person being tested has a weak field, the muscles will be weak and the person doing the testing will have an easier time pushing down her arm.

For example, let us start by muscle testing my friend Moira. When she says *"I am a woman"*, this causes her field to become strong, because her subconscious mind agrees with the statement that she is a woman. So, if she holds out her arm and says *"I am a woman"*, her field will go strong and make her muscles strong, and it will be more difficult for me to push her arm down.

Muscle testing, weak field

But, when she says *"I am a man"*, this causes her field to become weak, because her subconscious mind knows that she is not a man. So, if she holds out her arm and says *"I am a man"*, her field will go weak and make her muscles weak, and I will have an easier time pushing down her arm. Thus, it is possible to use muscle testing to quickly and effectively determine exactly what programs are or are not held in our subconscious software.

Four Methods of Muscle Testing

There are many methods of muscle testing. It is possible to muscle test in ways which isolate the various organ systems and parts of the body, and thereby determine where there are weaknesses or problems to be addressed. In fact, there is an entire discipline known as applied kinesiology that uses the technique of muscle testing as a method of diagnosing problems in the body.

However, for our purposes we are only interested in testing the body as a whole. This is very simple and easy to do. Four different methods of muscle testing will be described below, and each has its advantages and disadvantages. Also, every person is different, and some people find that they test much better with one method rather than the others. Everyone is encouraged to explore all of these methods and any others that you come across. Not only is muscle testing extremely useful, it is also a lot of fun!

While the information presented below should be sufficient to allow most people to start muscle testing easily, anyone who desires to learn more is encouraged to check out the Theta Healing LA Muscle Testing DVD, which provides live demonstrations of all of the four muscle testing methods described below. More information on the companion DVD and other healing resources can be found on the Theta Healing LA Web site at *www.Theta HealingLA.com.*

Muscle Testing Method #1: The Arm Lever

The arm lever test is extremely popular and has been adopted by many chiropractors and other alternative medicine practitioners. This test is performed by having the client hold out his arm to the side and resist as the practitioner pushes down on his arm. If the arm stays strong, the test result is true; if the arm goes weak and drops, the test result is false.

The advantages of the arm lever test are as follows:

- It is extremely fast to learn.
- It generally provides clear results without requiring a lot of practice.

- People who insist on muscle testing with all their strength to be convinced that it is real tend to like the arm lever test.
- It makes a great demonstration for a group because it is obvious to everyone whether the arm is going down or staying strong.

The disadvantages to the arm lever test include:

- It requires two people and cannot be done on your own.
- It takes a lot of energy and puts a lot of strain on the shoulder. It can only be used a limited number of times before the shoulder tires.

Muscle Testing Method #2: The Standing Test

Another method of muscle testing is the standing test. This is a great test because nearly everybody can do the standing muscle test right away without any training or practice. When we do the standing test, we essentially turn our body into a pendulum lever. If we stand and muscle test and feel our body tilting or being pushed forward, it means the result is strong, or TRUE. If we stand and feel our body tilting or being pushed backward, it means the result is weak, or FALSE.

To perform the standing muscle test, stand with your feet a little bit narrower than shoulder width apart. Stand facing towards magnetic north in a balanced, neutral position. Make sure you are standing very tall, with no bend in your knees. Keep your head and shoulders held high while remaining comfortable and relaxed (no pulling or straining). The feeling you want is that your upper body and head are "floating" on top of your legs. Also, be sure that your toes are pointed straight forward. If your toes are rotated outwards or inwards it will influence the test and it will be harder for you to get a consistent, accurate result.

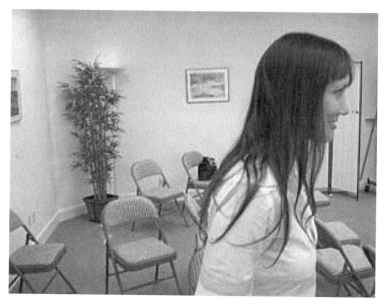

Standing muscle test, true result

While it is not strictly necessary to be facing magnetic north, it does help to get a clearer result. The standing test will give you an accurate result no matter which direction you are facing, but the result will be clearer if you can face to the north.

To test, stand tall, legs straight, shoulders and head held high, with your toes pointed straight forward, and say "*YES*" – you should feel yourself tilting forward.

Standing muscle test, false result

Next, rebalance yourself, and say *"NO"* – you should feel yourself tilting backwards. Some people experience this as a tilt where they are falling forwards or backwards, while other people experience this as a feeling of a magnetic push or pull forwards or backwards.

The advantages to the standing test include:

- Nearly everyone can get accurate testing results right away without much practice.
- It does not require another person, so you can use it to test yourself anytime and anywhere.
- It makes a great demonstration and is useful for muscle testing groups of people all at once because it is easy to see whether someone is moving forwards or backwards.

The main disadvantage of the standing test is that it cannot be used on people who have difficulty standing.

Muscle Testing Method #3: The Finger Ring

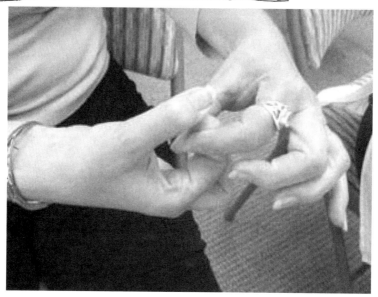

Finger ring test, true result

The finger ring test is a popular form of muscle testing because it requires very little energy and puts little or no strain on the body. The ring test can also be done on yourself, or with a partner. The instructions below will describe how to use the finger ring test to test yourself; if you wish to use this test with a partner, the only difference is that your partner will pull apart your fingers instead of you doing it yourself with your other hand.

To do the finger ring muscle test, sit in a relaxed, comfortable position. Make a ring with your thumb and one of your fingers (different people like to use different fingers; generally the pinky finger/thumb ring is the weakest, and the index finger/thumb ring is the strongest.) Hold the ring tight, and say *"YES"* as you use the index finger on your other hand to pull through the ring – the ring should stay intact.

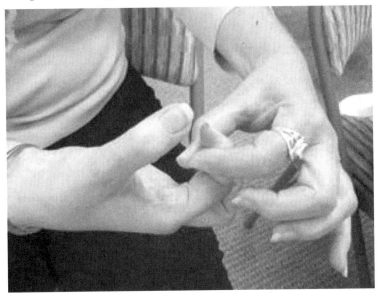

Finger ring test, false result

Hold the ring tight again, and this time say *"NO"* as you use the index finger on your other hand to pull through the ring – the ring should break and let your finger pull through. Advantages of the finger ring test include:

- It can be done at nearly any time and place, including a car, an airplane, or standing in line at the grocery store.
- It can be done with people who are not able to stand.
- It requires very little energy and puts very little strain on the body, and so it is possible to do dozens or hundreds of finger ring tests in a session.
- It does not require a partner and can be used to muscle test yourself.
- When done with a partner, nearly everyone is able to get clear and accurate results immediately.

Disadvantages of the finger ring test include:

- Most people require some practice before they can accurately test themselves using this method.
- It does not make a good demonstration for a group because it can be difficult to see whether or not the fingers stay together or pull apart during the test.

Muscle Testing Method #4: Pendulums

Using a pendulum is another form of muscle testing. A pendulum is simply a weight suspended on some sort of string or rope. To use a pendulum, you hold it in your hand and then say or think whatever it is that you wish to muscle test. The pendulum will rotate or swing one way or the other, depending on whether or not your subconscious mind agrees or disagrees with your statement.

For many people, if you hold a pendulum and then say something that resonates true with the subconscious mind, the pendulum will rotate clockwise. For example, if I say *"I am a man"* while holding my pendulum, it will rotate in the clockwise direction.

Similarly, if you hold a pendulum and then say something that resonates false with the subconscious mind, the pendulum will rotate counterclockwise. For example, if I say *"I am a woman"* while holding my pendulum, it will rotate in the counterclockwise direction.

There are many kinds of pendulums available. Personally, I prefer to use a light weight wood pendulum on a string. You can also use pendulums made of metal or crystals or all sorts of other materials. In a pinch, your key ring can serve as an ad-hoc pendulum. There are many different opinions and schools of thought about pendulums, including both how to make them and how to use them.

It typically requires some amount of practice to become proficient at using a pendulum. Additionally, pendulums can be influenced by outside energies, so it is important to regularly clear the pendulum of any energy other than our own, and to synchronize it to your body so that it will test clearly for you. People who have used pendulums recognize that a pendulum "gets to know you", and the more you practice with a particular pendulum, the easier and clearer the results will be.

Advantages of using the pendulum test include:

- It does not require a partner.
- It usually provides a clear result.
- Pendulums are easy to make and cheap to buy.

Disadvantages of using the pendulum test include:

- Most people require practice and familiarity with a particular pendulum before they can get consistently clear results with it.
- It does not make a good demonstration because it can be difficult for a group to see the result of the pendulum test.
- Pendulums can be influenced by energy other than your own.

Troubleshooting Muscle Testing

While most people can muscle test clearly and easily without needing much practice, some people may have difficulty with it.

Fortunately, there are several things you can do to help clear up the muscle test results.

The primary reason that most people do not test clearly is simple dehydration. Another common cause is demineralization (not enough minerals in the body). Why is this? Muscle testing is an electrical phenomenon, and electricity moves through the body via minerals suspended in water. So, if you do not have enough water or enough minerals in your body, it is more difficult for the electricity to flow, making muscle testing less reliable.

The first thing to do when you have trouble muscle testing is to drink plenty of water. Filtered and/or structured water works best, but just about any form of water will help to hydrate the body and improve the muscle test results. However, be careful when drinking distilled water, because distilled water can leach minerals out of the body and make it more difficult to muscle test clearly.

Getting enough water may seem like a really simple thing, but a good portion of our population (some will say as high as 70%) is dehydrated most of the time! It is certainly possible that you may need to drink several glasses of water to get hydrated well enough to muscle test. After drinking water, you can also hold your hands over your kidneys for 30 seconds or so to stimulate hydration through the body. Vianna calls this the "pregnant woman pose", since it is similar to how pregnant women will hold their hands on their back to provide support. Note, however, that the kidneys are up higher in the back than many people realize. In most people, the kidneys are up at about the level of the lowest (bottom) rib. Usually, drinking some water and holding the hands on the kidneys for 30 seconds helps most people to start muscle testing clearly.

Another technique to help get clearer muscle testing results is called "zipping the field." Our energy fields are affected by many things, including power lines, radiation from electronics, and other people's emotions. Sometimes our field can get little rips or distortions in it, which will make muscle testing more difficult. "Zipping the field" is a simple way to realign our energy field and fix these little tears and distortions. To zip, start with one hand directly in front of the center line of your body, down slightly beneath the root chakra (near the groin). Bring your hand up the center line of your body until it is over your head, and then bring your hand off to the side and let it relax. It is called "zipping the field" because the motion looks very much like zipping up a giant sleeping bag in which you are standing. (Be careful to bring your hand off to the side, and not back down the middle, after a zip, because if you bring your hand back down the middle of the body, you will unzip your field.)

Taking minerals can also help to clear up muscle tests. I personally prefer ionic minerals, which are in a chemical form that is easily absorbed and assimilated into the body. Taking the right form of minerals can help to provide clearer muscle tests.

There are several other things that can also help to clear up a stubborn muscle test. Sometimes it is helpful to apply 30 seconds of gentle pressure to the sub-occipital region of the head, which is near the bony bumps on the bottom of the back of the skull. It can also be helpful to take a pinch of salt, but I prefer to avoid suggesting this to clients, since not only is it unpleasant to eat salt directly, but also due to the interactions between dietary salt and blood pressure. Lastly, if you are a practitioner of Theta Healing, you can use the Theta technique itself to help to teach the body how to muscle test.

What Muscle Testing Can and Can Not Do

There are a number of fun and practical things that we can do with muscle testing. However, it is important to remember that **muscle testing is only checking the subconscious mind.** Muscle testing results are not necessarily the same as universal truth! Muscle testing only taps into the intelligence of the subconscious mind via the body, which may or may not be the same as the truth.

An example of a proper use of muscle testing is to check for the subconscious program *"I have to be poor to be close to God."* Why? Because we are asking the subconscious mind, via the muscles, if it contains a program that says you must be poor to be close to God.

An improper use of muscle testing would be to use it to figure out the next set of winning lottery numbers. You may get clear results, but you probably will not win the lottery, because the numbers you get are only the body's opinion of what the winning lottery numbers will be. Winning lottery numbers are an objective, external truth that has nothing to do with the programs running inside your subconscious software. As a result, the muscle test results are unlikely to be accurate. If I could actually use muscle testing in this way, I would have already won the lottery several times! But you don't have to take my word for it; instead, go muscle test the next set of winning lottery numbers, buy a ticket, and lose a dollar to convince yourself that it does not work.

The subconscious mind is extremely smart, and in fact it knows a lot more than the conscious mind, because the subconscious mind is in touch with other parts of us that cannot be directly accessed by the conscious mind. For example, Vianna teaches that we carry in our DNA all the experiences of all of our genetic ancestors back seven generations! (This does not mean that we cannot hold a genetic memory from more than seven generations past; it is just that we keep **every** experience and memory from the previous seven generations.) Obviously, most of us cannot consciously access these memories, but they are held in the subconscious mind and they do affect us. Hence, you can accurately query these memories with muscle testing.

The subconscious mind is also in touch with memories from other times and places – beyond those of our ancestors - which we collectively refer to as "past life memories." (It is not important to accept the theory of past lives or reincarnation to work with the subconscious or benefit from Theta Healing. However, it is important be open to the idea that it is possible for our subconscious minds to carry memories and experiences from other lifetimes.) These memories and experiences mesh with those of our current life and those of our genetic ancestors, giving our subconscious mind access to much greater knowledge and experience than the conscious mind. But no matter how smart our subconscious mind may be, it is not perfect, and it does not know everything.

Checking for Past Life Memories

One of the most fun things to do with muscle testing is to check to see what past life memories you hold. And it is easy! Using the muscle testing procedures described here, muscle test yourself for things such as:

- I was a samurai warrior.
- I was a healer.
- I was a doctor.
- I was a man.

- I was a woman.
- I was a King.
- I was a Queen.
- I was a peasant farmer.
- I lived in ancient Rome.
- I lived in ancient Greece.
- I lived in ancient Egypt.

Your imagination is the limit! You can also muscle-test yourself to see if you have known people in past lives. You might check the following tests for your parents, children, siblings, friends, and coworkers:

- I knew <name> in a past life.
- <name> was my husband.
- <name> was my wife.
- <name> was my child.
- <name> was my friend.
- <name> was my lover.
- <name> was my brother.
- <name> was my sister.
- <name> was my boss.

Checking for Old Vows, Oaths, Contracts, and Obligations

We have a saying that "You cannot take it with you." Well, that is only partially true. While it may be true that we cannot take our material possessions with us after our death, we do seem to carry certain aspects of our subconscious programming with us between lifetimes. This can sometimes result in us carrying old limiting vows, oaths, contracts, or other obligations that we took on in other times and places but still affect us today. You can use muscle testing to determine if you are carrying these sorts of things in your subconscious mind.

Because we carry our subconscious software with us after we die, I joke that some day in the future I am going to track down the future selves of my clients and send them bills!

A few common limiting obligations that people often carry from other times and places include the following:

- I have a Vow of Poverty.
- I have a Vow of Chastity.
- I have a Vow of Obedience.
- I have a Vow of Silence.
- I have Vows, Oaths, Contracts, or other Obligations to the Church/Templars/etc.
- I have Marriage Vows (other than to your current spouse.)

If you are having trouble with money in your life, and you are carrying a vow of poverty in your subconscious mind, you probably want to get rid of it.

Muscle Testing for Food and Supplements

Although muscle testing is widely used by practitioners of alternative health modalities to check which foods and supplements are best for a person, I do not use muscle testing for this purpose. Muscle testing only gives you the body's subconscious opinion as to whether or not a food or supplement is good for you, which may or not be the truth.

Now, sometimes this subconscious opinion will be the truth, and if you have no other method of determining what foods or supplements to pick, muscle testing may be better than blind guessing. But, there are circumstances where doing so can lead you astray. I have worked with many clients who are suspicious of muscle testing and carry what I call "pendulum trauma" because they previously worked with people who used muscle testing improperly.

For example, say that you are at the health food store and there are 20 different kinds of calcium on the shelf. Unfortunately, you have no way to know which one of them is going to be best for your body. So, you start muscle testing them, and you find that your muscle test result for the calcium in the orange bottle makes you go extremely strong. In fact, muscle testing the calcium in the orange bottle makes your muscle go noticeably stronger than any of the other bottles of calcium.

Does this mean that the calcium in the orange bottle is the best one for you to take? Well, it might be, but it also might not! It all depends on why your subconscious mind thinks that it is good for you. In fact, it may be that you are carrying a genetic memory of a time when one of your ancestors was extremely sick, until somebody came and gave them medicine out of an orange bottle. The medicine worked, and now you are carrying the subconscious programming in your DNA memories that things that come in orange bottles are good for your health. So, when you muscle test the calcium in the orange bottle, your test is extremely strong. But is it strong because this brand of calcium is particularly good for you, or simply because you believe that things in orange bottles are good for you?

If you wish to use muscle testing to check foods or supplements, it is a simple matter of holding it to your chest and performing any of the muscle testing methods described below. If your muscle test result is strong, it means that your subconscious mind believes that this food or supplement is good for you to take. Likewise, if the muscle test result is weak, it means that your subconscious mind believes that this is not a good food supplement for you. But remember that muscle testing results are not always the same as universal truths, so it is probably not a great idea to rely on muscle testing to choose supplements, or pick foods, or decide where to live, or who to marry, or anything of that sort. Fortunately, there are other techniques for accurately choosing the foods and supplements that will be best, and one such technique is taught in Theta Healing seminars.

Proxy Muscle Testing

Once you have practiced muscle testing yourself, it is possible to use the same technique to proxy for another person. By doing this, you can effectively use your body to muscle test for other people (and animals!) and check what their subconscious opinion is. This is the same process used by Theta Healing practitioners for clients who are not able to muscle test using the traditional methods, typically because the client is an animal, a small child, or a person who is in a coma or otherwise disabled. This is known as *proxy muscle testing*.

Essentially, performing a proxy muscle test uses your own energy field as a proxy for the field of another person or other being. Practitioners find that the proxy testing is not as accurate as direct testing, but it is a great option for situations where direct testing is not possible.

Doing proxy muscle testing for another person is a potential violation of their privacy, so it is recommended that you only proxy test for others with their permission.

Any of the above methods of muscle testing can be easily adapted for proxy muscle testing. The only difference is that instead of making a statement to test your own subconscious mind, you test another's subconscious mind by prefacing your statement with *proxy for <whomever>*. If I muscle test for myself the statement "*I am a cat*", then I expect the result to be FALSE, or weak, because I am a human being. But if I were to do a proxy muscle test for my cat Callisto and say "*Proxy for Callisto, I am a cat*", I expect the result to be TRUE, or strong, because my field is acting as a proxy for Callisto's field, which knows that she is a cat.

Similarly, if I were to muscle test the statement "*Proxy for Callisto, I am a human*", I expect the result to be FALSE. And if I want to proxy test for my cat Callisto to see if she knows me from a past life memory (it is common for our pets to return to us again and again across lifetimes), I would muscle test the statement "*Proxy for Callisto, I knew Brent in a past life*". (And yes she did!)

What does Muscle Testing Really Tell Us?

The subconscious mind – the software inside of us that manifests our reality – can be directly queried via the muscle testing technique. This means that with muscle testing we are able to see what is and what is not in the subconscious mind, giving us a tool to better understand how and why we create the various conditions and experiences in our life.

For example, if you are having trouble keeping money in your life, you may find that you are holding a subconscious vow of poverty. You can test this yourself by muscle testing the statement "*I have a vow of poverty.*" If the muscle test result is strong, or TRUE, it means that you are holding this vow in your subconscious… and you should probably get rid of it if you want to be able to attract and keep a lot of money!

Returning to the computer metaphor, knowing how to muscle test is like knowing enough about the computer to determine which applications are on it and what those applications can do, but not enough to know how to install new applications or how to modify the existing ones. This is useful, but you are limited to using only the programs that are already installed on your computer. So, if you want to use your computer for word processing, you better hope that there is a word processing program already installed. If not, you are out of luck.

Similarly, if there are bugs in the software on your computer, and you do not know how to reprogram the computer or install new software, there is nothing you can do about it except try to live with the bugs. For example, if your computer crashes every time you use your word processor to print something, you will have to live with rebooting your system every time you print… that. That is, at least until you learn how to fix the bug that is the source of the problem.

Somebody who does not know how to muscle test is like a novice computer user who does not even know how to determine what programs are installed on their computer. You can ask this person a lot of questions about the computer, but they cannot give you any meaningful answers because they just do not know what the computer can do or what software is on it. They also have no idea how to find these things out.

Using muscle testing to check yourself for your subconscious software is like knowing how to browse your computer to see which programs are installed on it. If you are working with a computer running Windows, it is a simple matter of clicking on the *Start* button and then clicking the *Programs* button to see what programs are available on the computer. Anybody who is familiar with Windows knows how to do this, and it is easily learned. But, somebody who does not have any knowledge or training with computers will think it is impossible for them.

This is just like the ability to directly check what programs are in the subconscious using muscle testing. It may initially seem crazy or impossible that we can easily determine what is in the subconscious mind, but once you know how to muscle test, you will see that it is actually quite simple, and even a lot of fun!

At this point you may be thinking "It is great to be able to determine what is in the subconscious mind, but what if I really want to be able to do something about it?" After all, even if you are able to accurately determine exactly what is in your subconscious mind, unless you are able to change it then you will still feel that you are a victim to the circumstances of your life. If the part of ourselves that is manifesting our reality – the subconscious software – seems impossible to change, then we will feel powerless to change our life experiences.

This is where a technique such as Theta Healing comes to the rescue: it allows us to fix the "bugs" that we find with muscle testing!

Chapter 5: The Four Levels of the Subconscious

"After one session with Theta I was able to walk without a brace!"

Brent, do not know where to begin, How about in the present THANK YOU!!! 6 months ago I twisted my ankle. "Experts" told me I tore ligaments & might have to go under the knife --- have surgery. (YUCK) Aside from the fact that I would spend copious amounts of money on healing I was terrified. After one session with Theta I was able to walk without a brace. For anyone who is at the end of the rope & truly wants to evoke CHANGE I Recommend Theta.

Brent, I cannot thank you enough, I want to share this info with everyone I meet. I will be calling you again to work on some other areas of my life that need healing. Thank you again.

MADISON M.
Beverly Hills, California

The "software" of the subconscious mind is the master blueprint for all the experiences you manifest in your life, whether it is for your health, finances, relationships, or even your spirituality. If you desire greater wealth in your life, the most effective solution is to reprogram your subconscious for a higher level of wealth. Similarly, if you are having a health challenge in our lives, clearing out all the subconscious reasons why this problem has manifested will help you to heal it. Before we can further explore how this is done, we need to explain the nature of the subconscious mind and how these negative programs get in there in the first place.

There are four levels where programs are held in our subconscious mind: the core level, the genetic level, the history level, and the soul level.

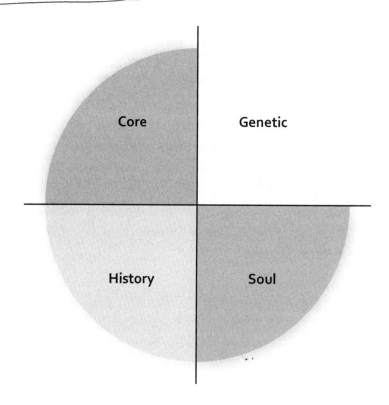

Four Levels of the Subconscious

The Core Level of the Subconscious

We all understand that we are deeply imprinted by the experiences of our childhood. The things that we are told and the experiences that we have as children, particularly as young children, shape us and have a huge impact on our lives and how we feel about things. Many people spend their entire lives running away from their childhood demons.

The reason that children – especially babies and infants – are so impressionable is that children are born in a theta brainwave, and stay in a predominantly theta brain state until approximately two years of age. It is therefore understandable how the things we experience very early in life is impressed directly upon the subconscious mind, and these impressions can profoundly affect us for the rest of our lives.

It is interesting to note that people who are able to remember their birth or events very early in childhood often make talented Theta Healing practitioners, because their brains are wired so that they can remember things even when in a deep theta brainwave. I know that my brain is wired to use a conscious theta brainwave because I actually remember being born, and have a few vivid (albeit brief) memories of being an infant.

We also carry subconscious programming from our time in the womb. From the moment of conception we are affected by the thoughts and emotions around us, and sometimes problems in our life are rooted in things that happened to our mother before we were born. Further, birth can be a traumatic and damaging experience, particularly if there was a problem with the birth (i.e. if forceps were used, or if the mother was given powerful drugs during labor or delivery.)

In addition to the time in the womb, birth, and the experiences of early childhood, it is possible to pick up core level programming at any time during our lives. We do not stop being influenced by the world around us just because we reach a certain age; instead, the world around us tends to influence us less and less over time, so that it takes more powerful experiences to make an impression upon an adult's subconscious mind. But things that happen in adulthood can certainly impact the subconscious mind, and a good deal of time is spent during Theta Healing sessions resolving core level issues that are not from childhood.

The Genetic Level of the Subconscious

One of the reasons that the subconscious mind has a greater awareness and intelligence than our conscious mind is that it is not limited to the experiences of just this lifetime. We carry far more information and influence than we realize in our DNA, which is like a giant computer code. Thus, the way that we feel, our health, our mood, our loves and fears, everything about our lives can be rooted in our DNA. If you had a grandmother six generations ago who was bitten by a spider and became extremely ill or died, you might be afraid of spiders (arachnophobia) and not understand why.

DNA Activation

There has also been much talk in the spiritual and New Age community on DNA activation. There are many books on the subject, and magazines such as the *Sedona Journal of Channeling*. They are full of articles about different techniques for DNA activation. In fact, one of the early applications of Theta Healing was to activate the DNA.

So what exactly is DNA activation?

The DNA that we know about in our body is just one of twelve strands, or layers, of the DNA. This first layer of the DNA, also known as the physical layer, is the familiar "double helix" shape that looks like a twisted ladder. Each "rung" on the ladder is composed of four chemical structures (commonly labeled A, G, T, and C). These make up the alphabet of our genetics. Effectively, the DNA is a binary code, a series of ones and zeroes that is quite similar to a computer code. (Gregg Braden's book *The God Code* explores the similarity of DNA and computer code.)

The DNA codes are organized into chromosomes, which come in pairs. Each chromosome consists of various genes, where each gene is a blueprint for making a certain protein. So, when you have a gene for something, it just means that you have a certain recipe somewhere in your DNA that tells your body how to make a protein. These proteins can have a powerful influence on our health and well-being. For example, the ability to make a certain protein may make you either immune or vulnerable to a certain disease. Many genetic disorders result in the body lacking the genes to make certain important proteins.

One of the applications of Theta Healing is working with the physical layer of the DNA, or the DNA that science knows about and that we can see in the body. However, there are also other energetic layers to the DNA that have been "turned off" in most humans. These energetic layers of the DNA cannot be seen under a microscope and until quite recently we were unaware of them.

There are a total of 12 layers of the DNA – 1 physical, and 11 energetic. The first layer of the DNA, the physical layer, is essentially a cookbook full of recipes for making different proteins. So, what are the other layers for and what do they do?

The short answer is that the other eleven energetic layers of the DNA are recipes for accessing the non-physical world, or "the other side of the veil." It is from there that our spirits come, and to where we return after we die; it is also the home of the energies we access for healings and manifestations. All the so-called psychic phenomena – including remote viewing, telepathy, instant healings, guardian angel readings, communicating with our ancestors, and future readings – have their codes in these energetic layers of the DNA. Just as the first (physical) layer of the DNA holds codes to make proteins, these energetic layers of the DNA provide the blueprints for the way we access guardian angels, ancestors, instant healings, and other so-called mystical abilities.

It is a simple matter to activate, or "turn on", these layers of the DNA, so that we can regain access to the multidimensional aspects of ourselves that have been lost for a very long time.

There is a large amount of literature about the activation of the DNA, of varying degrees of clarity and truth. Whatever else you may have heard about DNA activation and the 12 layers of the DNA, it is true that more and more people are learning to access their intuitive or psychic abilities. It is also far easier now to train people to do these things than it was just a few years back. Heck, just a handful of years ago I was a hard-core agnostic and scientist engineer who had no psychic ability whatsoever. Yet today, I am teaching people how to perform instant miraculous healings and psychic readings!

When performing the Theta Healing technique, part of what happens in the body when subconscious programs are changed and healing occurs are changes in the DNA. Although I personally have not worked with any clients with genetic diseases, Vianna and other Theta Healing practitioners have had amazing results using Theta Healing on genetic disorders, proving that something must really be happening to change the DNA. But, for the most part, we do not need to worry about the details of the DNA. Instead, the important thing to recognize here is that we are profoundly influenced by the genetic codes in our DNA. Therefore, an important part of the way that we change ourselves and reprogram our reality is to change our DNA.

The History Level of the Subconscious

Another way that we pick up subconscious programming is from events that occurred in other times and places. Whether or not you believe in past lives is not important; for our purposes, these "past life memories" are simply experiences from other times and places beyond our current lifetime that are somehow affecting us today.

We can be strongly influenced by these past life memories of events and experiences that have happened in other times and places. Some understand this as reincarnation, karma, tribal memories, or mass consciousness. But, for whatever reason, we do carry memories of these experiences within us. As a result, we can be greatly affected by them.

For example, have you ever met someone for the first time and felt a powerful emotional charge? It may have been great anger, or great love, yet you did not understand why you felt this way. The reason is that your feeling was not accessible to the conscious mind, but was instead hidden in the subconscious mind as a past life memory. Because our subconscious programming sponsors and creates our feelings, we sometimes have powerful feelings that we do not consciously understand. This can be particularly intense when it comes to interpersonal relationships, and we will discuss the influence of past life memory experiences on personal relationships – soul-mates – later in this book.

There is a great deal of misunderstanding about the concept of past lives. It is not important or even helpful to get into the dogma of whether we have one or many lives, or exactly how reincarnation or the afterlife works. (A more correct term for past lives would be parallel inter-dimensional experiences, but we will not delve any deeper into the metaphysics of multiple lifetimes here.) The important thing to recognize is that whether or not we were actually somebody else in a past life is far less important than whether or not the subconscious mind *thinks* that we were.

For example, say that your subconscious mind believes that you were Cleopatra, and that you are holding trauma from her death. (Cleopatra is known to have died from the bite of a poisonous snake.) As a result, you are afraid of snakes, and this past life memory needs to be addressed before the phobia can be released. It does not matter whether or not past lives are real, or whether or not you really were Cleopatra. What **does** matter is that you are holding subconscious programming that says that you should be afraid of snakes because you are carrying a memory of a painful death from a snake bite. Whether or not this is "objectively true", you will continue to be afraid of snakes until you clear that traumatic memory out of your subconscious software.

This explains why there are probably a million people out there who believe they were Cleopatra in a past life and will muscle test TRUE to *"I was Cleopatra."* For one, linear time does not exist on "the other side", so it is not only silly but also improper to impose a model of linear time on multiple lifetimes. For another, it is not necessary to have actually been Cleopatra to hold subconscious programming that says that you were her. Thus, the subconscious program *"I was Cleopatra"* could very well be held in your DNA because of a movie your grandmother watched.

Another common example of programs being held on the history level is a past life memory of being a healer. We can use muscle testing to check for the subconscious program *"It is safe for me to be a healer"*, and frequently the result is FALSE, because the subconscious mind is holding programs on the history level that say it is dangerous to be a healer. Many of us have memories of being healers who were punished for some type of healing. We all know about the witch hunts in the Middle Ages, as well as the Salem witch trials in America, where thousands were tortured and killed after being accused of performing witchcraft. Thus, many of us hold subconscious programming that it is dangerous to heal people or that if we heal, someone we will be killed for it. Obviously, very few of us have actually been punished for performing healings in our current lifetimes, but many of us are still affected by the memories of when this happened in other times and places.

Once again, it is important to emphasize that whether or not a memory held in the subconscious is "real" and actually happened is not important. Instead, what is truly important is what a person's subconscious believes regarding it. Thus, if a person believes in his subconscious that he was abused as a child and damaged as a result, he will tend to manifest experiences of being damaged. Whether or not the abuse actually occurred is far less important than his belief that it did.

Similarly, many people believe they were abducted by aliens, and are holding traumatic experiences in their subconscious as a result. Although it is far more likely that the cause of the trauma was not an alien abduction, but rather sexual abuse, the objective truth of the cause is not important. Instead, what is important is that these traumas (real or imagined) must be cleared out of the subconscious for the person to heal and transform his life for the better.

In Theta Healing terminology, the "history" level is the accumulation of all these programs from other people, times, and places. In the next chapter we discuss how to use Theta Healing in order to release the subconscious impact of these experiences level.

The Soul Level of the Subconscious

The fourth level on which we hold the subconscious programming is the soul level, which encompasses all we are in a divine perspective. The "soul" level involves issues such as our life and the most important things we come to live as a human on Earth to experience.

Of all the levels, we tend to work the least amount directly on the soul level, because it is generally more abstract, and its issues tend to manifest through the other levels, For example, if part of your soul's mission is to learn to overcome poverty, then you may choose to be born into an extremely poor family. This will provide you with many blocks to prosperity on the genetic level that must be cleared so that you can have an experience of overcoming poverty.

Still, the soul level is powerful and important, and one of the most powerful techniques of Theta Healing is the ability to actually heal *a broken soul*. A 'broken soul' occurs when we have experiences that are so intensely painful and difficult that the energy at the very core of our being fractures. People who spend their entire lives feeling broken or feeling that it is impossible for them be completely fixed often have broken souls. And, until the soul is fixed, the mind and body cannot be made whole.

Why the Subconscious Matters

The subconscious mind is so important because it is that part of us that creates all of our experiences in life. If you are holding negative programs in your subconscious, you will create and manifest negative experiences that fit your negative programs.

For example, if you believe that rich people are greedy, you will tend to manifest life experiences where rich people act greedy. These experiences will in turn support this belief. We call these experiences *validating evidence* for our beliefs.

This is an important but subtle point. Just because you have a lot of validating evidence for a certain subconscious program, does not make the belief absolutely true. If you are holding certain programs in your subconscious software, you need to recognize that they may very well seem true to you, but only because all of your experiences fit the underlying programs that are manifesting them.

Going back to our earlier example, if you hold the subconscious program that rich people are greedy, then you will tend to find that the rich people you interact with in your life often seem greedy – because your subconscious software is creating life experiences that fit your programming! It seems to you, therefore, that the program "rich people are greedy" is *objectively true*. Subconsciously held prejudices of this sort are powerful self-fulfilling prophecies.

Here is an example of how we may think something is true based on our experiences, even though it is not true in reality. Take a person who grew up on a farm in the country and woke up each morning before dawn. Each morning he witnessed darkness, heard a rooster crow and then witnessed the sun rise. Based on this experience, the person forms the belief that "when the cock crows, the sun will rise." Although his experience tells him that this is true, we know that the fact that the rooster crows has absolutely nothing to do with whether or not the sun rises.

Fortunately, when we are able to identify the effect of certain negative programs in our subconscious, there are various ways that we can change our subconscious software to "fix the bugs" and change our life experiences.

How We Can Reprogram Our Subconscious Software

Theta Healing is an incredibly powerful and easy to utilize tool to reprogram the subconscious, but it is far from the only way. Before we start a discussion of how to use Theta Healing to directly work with the subconscious, it is valuable to review some of the other common ways that we can reprogram our subconscious software.

Life Experience Impacts Our Subconscious Programming

Every time we have a life experience, some part of that experience imprints upon our subconscious. There are a variety of factors that determine how deeply and powerfully these experiences are imprinted upon us. For example, we are all familiar with the fact that powerful experiences early in childhood can have a profound and transforming effect upon us. These experiences can strongly affect us for the rest of our lives, whereas perhaps a similar experience later in life would not be such a big deal.

Every time that we have an interaction with someone who is rich, it affects all of our programs, judgments, experiences, and expectations for all the other rich people in the world. This is because the brain acts like a giant connection machine, always looking for connections between different pieces of data. If we have an experience with a certain person who acts a certain way, then we may connect that person's behavior with everyone else who is like them. Therefore, if we have a business lunch with a rich person who is also Hispanic and bald, our experiences during that lunch will influence our subconscious programming about not only rich people but also Hispanic people and bald people. Similarly, if you are attacked by a dog when you are a young child, you may develop a fear of all dogs, though of course not all dogs have attacked you – only the one!

This tends to happen in a particularly powerful fashion with romantic relationships. It is common for a person to have a bad experience with someone, and generalize it to believe things like *"All men are pigs"* or *"All women hate me."* Sadly, if you take on this sort of belief, you will continue to manifest experiences that fit your beliefs, providing more and more validating evidence that supports your beliefs. And, each time you have a new experience that supports your prejudices and expectations, it makes it that much harder to change.

This generalization of behavior is amazingly powerful because it is extremely primitive and central to our being. It is not all bad, though, because it also serves to keep us alive and safe. For example, say you were a primitive human child living in the wild, and the first time you saw a wolf your parents told you to stay away from it because the wolf is a dangerous creature. After that you did not need to learn from personal experience that every individual wolf is dangerous, because our brains can "pattern match" to generalize our experiences and learn abstract lessons from them.

The downside of this powerful pattern matching behavior is that it is extremely common for the human brain to over generalize and take on programming that really does not make a lot of sense. Many of the divisions in the world today caused by racism can find their roots in such overgeneralizations. Because the subconscious mind has the power to manifest life according to the programming inside of us, it is easy for people to get caught up in the cycle of traumas and negative experiences that are over-generalized. For example, if you hold subconscious programming that all people of race X are stupid and greedy, then you will tend to manifest life experiences that support your subconscious programs and it will appear to you that people of race X really are stupid and greedy. Hence, this gives you "proof" that your prejudice is justified and objectively true.

Our Thoughts Impact Our Subconscious Programming

One of the most important ways that we change our subconscious programming is by changing the thoughts we have. It may not seem at first that our thoughts are under our control, but indeed they are (at least to a certain extent). We **do**, in fact, control the kinds of things about which we think – *especially* how much time we think about certain experiences or aspects of our lives.

There are innumerable self-help books and programs that talk about the power of positive thinking, and how important it is to change your thoughts to change your life experiences. All of these various programs and protocols rely upon the same underlying truth: that the thoughts you think will powerfully impact your subconscious mind, and hence change the kind of life experiences you have. One of the best known examples is the DVD and accompanying book *The Secret*, which postulates that if you can change the focus of your thinking, your whole life will improve, via the Law of Attraction.

In 1995 everything was going my way: I had a great education from MIT, I was a world's expert on Internet programming, and the great Internet boom of the 1990s was just starting. Yet, a short time later I had lost everything. I could not work, I was broke, I was in constant pain, and the best doctors were telling me that I could never recover. When my life was shattered by repetitive stress injuries that caused me to lose my career as a software engineer, I felt like a complete loser. I had been on top of the world, and yet I had completely screwed it up and ended up with nothing. Naturally, I got really down on myself and constantly berated myself as a hopeless case. In fact, I labeled myself an "Epic Loser" because I saw how enormous was the transition from my life being amazing and full of incredible potential to losing everything with no hope of ever recovering. For me, my failures were more spectacular and awful than most regular, run-of-the-mill losers could achieve.

And guess what happened after I starting telling myself that I was a loser? It sank into my subconscious mind! In fact, I had installed into myself new subconscious software that ran the program *"I am a complete loser."* As a result, I began manifesting life experiences that fit this new programming. No matter what I did, my health continued to get worse. And no matter how hard I tried to restart my career, everything I did failed miserably. Even after the terrible health crisis, I still had several opportunities to hit it big during the Internet gold rush. I had some amazing ideas, great technology, and slick business plans, but nothing I did was ever successful. Over and over I was on the verge of licensing my technology or achieving funding for a new company, but every time disaster struck and I was left with nothing. And despite spending years and many tens of thousands of dollars on both conventional and alternative health care therapies, my health only continued to get worse.

Why? In retrospect, I understand what happened. Because I was continually telling myself that I was a complete loser who would never achieve any success and that I would never recover my health, those programs got embedded into my subconscious software. And as a result, I manifested exactly those experiences: I did not have any success and I did not recover my health. And until I was able to use Theta Healing to fix those bugs in my subconscious, nothing I did was able to bring me any degree of success or improved health.

If you have had a lot of terrible things happen to you, it is very easy to get down on yourself, the world, and everyone around you. If you have recently suffered the typical humiliations of a country western song (that is, if you lost your job, had your wife leave you for your best friend, had your house burn down, had your truck stolen and had your dog run away all before breakfast) then it is completely understandable that you might start saying to yourself *"I am a loser."* But if you dwell on this thought as well as all the negative aspects of yourself, all the mistakes you have made and all the things you regret about your life, you will be strongly imprinting that negative programming upon your subconscious mind!

And guess what happens when you get mired in negative thinking? You start making those negative programs more and more powerful in your subconscious, which then starts creating negative life experiences to serve as validating evidence for those programs. If you continue to be down on yourself and tell yourself all the time that you are a loser, then at some point these thoughts are going to get installed into the subconscious software and you will start manifesting and creating life experiences to give you evidence that you are a loser. This validating evidence will only make you believe more and more strongly that you are a loser, and, the more you believe it, the more experiences you will have confirming it, perpetuating the cycle *ad infinitum.*

The way to break the cycle is extremely simple, though it may not always be easy: you just need to change your thinking. However, this is rarely a simple matter of will power. Our thinking is powerfully influenced by our feelings, which are created out of our subconscious software. If we are overwhelmed by powerful feelings, we may not be able to help but feel a certain way and think about certain negative things all the time, making it seem impossible to start thinking positively.

As with the example of the country western song, you may be so overwhelmed by grief that when all these terrible things happen to you, you feel so much pain and anguish that you cannot help but think negative thoughts. In this case, you need to be able to fix the subconscious bugs to relieve the intensity of those terrible feelings that are forcing you to think so negatively. No matter how justified your negative thinking may be, it does not change the fact that it is creating and manifesting even more negative circumstances and experiences in your life. But as long as the emotional volume on your pain and despair is high, it will be impossible to think differently. Instead, you first need to work with the subconscious to turn down the emotional volume of your despair and negativity to give yourself a fighting chance to think more positively. Positive thinking seminars and Law of Attraction coaches tell us that we have to change our thinking to change our lives. But this is often easier said than done, because when we are overcome by powerful emotions we become truly helpless to change how we are thinking.

We tend to think "when things get better, I will change how I think", but it does not work this way. You have to change how you think before life sends you positive experiences, because your experiences are just reflections of your thinking and subconscious programming. If you really want to have some validating evidence for positive thoughts, you first have to find some way to reverse your negative thinking and start thinking positively!

If you do not have access to techniques that are effective in changing how you feel and think, it is very easy to get mired in this negative thinking for a very long time, maybe even your whole life.

Fortunately, Theta Healing can shift the subconscious programming that causes these terrible feelings. We can release the pain and trauma, giving ourselves a chance to think positively and experience better lives, possibly for the first time in our memory. I remember that after my first session of Theta Healing with Terry I told her "Terry, for the first time in my life, I think it is now actually possible for me to think positively."

Whatever it takes, you must find a way to replace your destructive negative thoughts with positive thoughts if you wish for your life experiences to improve. All thoughts imprint upon our subconscious, and your negative thinking will continuously put new negative programs into your subconscious. Fortunately, when you are able to reverse the negative thinking, your new, positive thinking will constantly reinforce your positive subconscious programming and you will manifest validating evidence of wonderful and amazing life experiences of health, wealth, and happiness!

Affirmations and Mantras for Reprogramming the Subconscious

Our thinking and our experiences are not the only way we can change our subconscious software. There are also various active techniques to change our subconscious programming, and one of the easiest, oldest, and most commonly used is the technique of affirmations or mantras. By repeatedly stating a certain affirmation or mantra, it is possible to imprint new subconscious programming upon ourselves.

Repeated affirmations are one form of positive thinking, enhanced by the inherent power of carefully selected words. By speaking certain words, you are sending out into the Universe vibrations that support what you are saying by reinforcing subconscious programming within yourself. For example, if you repeatedly chant the mantra *"I love my neighbor"*, you will begin to install subconscious programming that says that you love your neighbor. As a result, you will likely start to manifest positive life experiences of friendship between you and your neighbors.

Affirmations and mantras are common and simple techniques for creating life changes by reprogramming the subconscious. However, be sure that you are reinforcing the right programming!

First, it is extremely important to state all your declarations, affirmations, and other mantras in the present tense as statements of the moment and what is already so.

To see how this can be important, let us examine a few common mistakes that people make with prayers and other affirmations. Let us pretend for a moment that you get to make one prayer, and for this one prayer you have a hot line that goes directly to God. Not only that, you are guaranteed that God will give you exactly what you pray for! So you think to yourself,

"Okay self, this is great... let's ask for a lot of money – let's get a million dollars!" So you then reach out and pick up a hotline and tell God, *"I want a million dollars!"*

What happens as a result? It is probably not what you expect! When you make the affirmation *"I want a million dollars"*, what you are actually creating or manifesting is the circumstance of wanting a million dollars. So, God says "Hallelujah, it is a miracle, your prayer is granted: **you want a million dollars!"**

Ouch, eh? When you have manifested *wanting* a million dollars, you have in fact prevented yourself from ever *having* a million dollars. Why? Because as long as God is granting your prayer of wanting a million dollars, he will not let you have a million dollars. If you had it, then you would stop wanting it; and God is not going to let you stop wanting it, because he is graciously granting your clearly stated prayer of "I **want** a million dollars."

To make your prayers, affirmations, and mantras effective, avoid words like "want" and simply word your affirmations, prayers, and mantras as statements of *what is already so*. This way you will program your subconscious with the right signals. The "right" thing to have said over the hotline to God is *"I have a million dollars now"*, as this will manifest the condition of having a million dollars!

To take this a step further, an even better affirmation is to say "I have at least a million dollars now." Why? If the Universe is trying to bring you two million dollars, but you are only asking for a million, you may not get the money because you explicitly stated that you have one million dollars rather than two. This is similar to what happens in Shakespeare's play *The Merchant of Venice*, where Shylock was entitled to his pound of flesh, but not one iota more or less.

Another common mistake with prayers and affirmations is the use of time. The brain does not really understand time. Although it roughly understands the idea of the past, the present, and the future, because the past has already happened and the future has not happened yet, the brain really only considers what is happening now in the moment. Thus, any time you make a statement of the form *"I will do 'X' in the future"*, it will not strongly imprint upon the subconscious, because the subconscious discards it as being less important because it is in the future. So, if you really wish to call wealth into your life, do not state that *"I will be rich."* Instead, state *"I am rich now!"*

For example, if you say a prayer or affirmation that that you will have a million dollars in six months on January 1, then on January 2, you will still be manifesting the condition of having a million dollars in six months... and on July 1 (six months after the deadline of your original prayer), you will still be manifesting the condition of having a million dollars in six months. Ouch! Better to put all your prayers and affirmations in the now, as statements of what is already so. This is what is meant by the Bible verse "Therefore, I tell you, all the things you pray and ask for believe that you have received them, and you will have them (Mark 11:24)."

Visualization for Reprogramming the Subconscious

Another powerful way that we can influence our subconscious programming and change the experiences we manifest is through visualization and imagination. Scientists now recognize that in terms of our brain chemistry and how experiences impact us, there is no difference between actually having an experience and simply imagining it! It has been proven experimentally that the brain reacts in an identical fashion whether we actually experience something, or merely imagine it. Therefore, whether something is actually happening to you or you are simply imagining it, the effect upon the brain and the subconscious will be the same.

Hence, in the same way that our thoughts and experiences impact and modify our subconscious programming, the things we imagine and visualize will also powerfully influence us.

The 1960s cartoon *The Jetsons* was set in a futuristic high tech world where one of the "advances" of the future was that people did not actually need to exercise anymore. Instead, they would simply watch a video of themselves exercising on a TV screen, and would get the benefit of the exercise. Of course, in the cartoon this was meant as a joke, but it contains a powerful kernel of truth.

Athletes know this, and this is why so many successful athletes perform visualization exercises to enhance their practice and prepare for competitions. The body can only tolerate so much physical training during a day, so there is a limit to how much preparation can be done by the physical practice of a particular sport. However, while the body is recovering, athletes can use their minds to visualize practicing and being successful in a sport, and continue to reinforce the positive programming in the subconscious.

Here is a great illustration of how this works. If you are an Olympic weightlifter, of course it is important to work out and eat right and do all of the traditional training. But in addition, you will likely find it valuable to do visualization exercises where you imagine yourself lifting heavier weights and imagine your muscles growing stronger. This will install subconscious programming that you are growing stronger, and this will in turn cause you to actually be stronger and lift heavier weights.

This is not just some obscure scientific theory; go ask any serious athlete and they will tell you that visualization really works!

There was a study done many years back where they took two groups of basketball players. One group performed 100 actual free throws while the second group only visualized making 100 free throws. Then, they were measured on how many free throws they were able to make after the warm up. The results were amazing: there was no measurable difference between the two groups! Both realized the same improvements, meaning that this experiment showed that visualization can be just as powerful as actual practice.

Other Ways of Reprogramming the Subconscious

There are many other ways that we can work with the subconscious, some more direct than others. Various self-help books talk about the power of the subconscious mind, and offer exercises such as writing letters to ourselves as techniques to help imprint new programming upon the subconscious software.

One such technique is a form of aversion therapy. If you have negative subconscious programs you want to purge, one technique that some people have used is to cause yourself some form of momentary but harmless pain (such as snapping yourself with a rubber band) whenever you think about something negative. So, if you are having trouble quitting drinking, you might start snapping yourself with a rubber band every time you think about drinking to create an association of pain with drinking to help you to quit. (Personally, I do not do this, as there are faster and better ways to clear the subconscious bugs without inflicting pain on yourself.)

There are many similar techniques of varying degrees of effectiveness that all have a few traits in common. For one, they are all indirect ways of accessing the subconscious – such as visualizing or using some external stimulus like pain – in the hope that it will create some sort of permanent and measurable change in the subconscious software. Saying mantras, going to 12 step meetings, and doing visualization exercises are great, but they are all still indirect methods of working with the subconscious mind.

Another trait that all of these techniques have in common is that they do not let you clearly know when a certain negative subconscious program has been released. For example, if you find yourself always thinking that rich people are greedy, you may realize that you are holding the subconscious program *"Rich people are greedy"* and want to get rid of it. So, you start snapping yourself on the wrist with a rubber band every time you think that rich people are greedy. But when do you get to stop? Of course you do not want to snap yourself on the wrist more times than you have to, but at the same time you do not want to stop if the subconscious programming has not changed yet. If you snap yourself on the wrist 1,000 times and then the program changes in your subconscious, you may continue to snap yourself thousands of times more, causing yourself unnecessary pain, because you do not know for certain when the program is cleared.

Theta Healing and muscle testing address both these issues. Theta is a direct technique of working with the subconscious, and uses muscle testing to quickly and quantitatively identify not only what negative programs are in the subconscious, but also when they are gone. So, if you are holding the subconscious program *"Rich people are greedy"* and you work on it with Theta

Healing and recheck the muscle test, you may find that the program is gone. Then you know for certain that you can stop worrying about it and move on to other things!

The Influence of Brainwaves on the Subconscious

Why is it that some experiences simply wash off of us, and others which are much less intense or important stick with us forever? The answer seems to be that the degree to which an experience influences the subconscious depends largely upon the brainwaves of that person when the experience occurs. In particular, the slower the brainwaves (especially theta) that a person has, the more powerfully an experience will influence them in their subconscious software.

As previously discussed, an important reason that children, particularly young children, are so impressionable is because they naturally have a large amount of theta brainwave activity. Even older children tend to retain a lot more theta and alpha brainwave activity compared with adults. Thus, it makes sense that the things that happen to us as children impact us more deeply in the subconscious.

All of the techniques discussed above for changing the subconscious work much more quickly and much more powerfully when the brain is in a theta state. In fact, the entire discipline of Hypnosis is based upon this principle. By using certain techniques to hypnotize a person, the brainwaves can be lowered to the theta state so the hypnotist can then directly access and work with that person's subconscious software.

Is There a Better Way to Reprogram the Subconscious?

Are you asking yourself, "Is there a better way that we can quickly and easily make profound changes in the subconscious mind?"

If so, the answer is a resounding **yes**: Theta Healing!

Chapter 6: Reprogramming the Subconscious Mind with Theta Healing

"No symptoms, nothing, I imagine that that is how anyone else might feel after an aerobic activity."

I have had asthma for as long as I can remember. As a child I can remember being hospitalized many, many times for this disease, and going in to the doctor countless others. For years I carried around inhalers just in case I had an attack. It seemed like something I would just have to live with, and that would probably be with me for the rest of my life. I knew this because it ran in the family: my uncle has had chronic asthma since he was young, and my brother had it as well. There is no cure for this disease.

During extreme weather changes, I am prone to getting very sick, and this generally triggers the asthma which makes both worse. It has had me in the emergency room twice, from apparent contact to a small animal pet bedding that is very dusty. I got two new inhalers, one I kept in the car, the other with me. This is all that modern technology can do for me: suppress the symptoms once they start.

[I had a phone session with Brent and] he told me he thought I would see some immediate improvement, though he warned me "I would not go out and run laps or anything." Half an hour or so later I really did feel good, so I decided to test it. I hopped on my bike and took a 2 mile ride, controlled my breathing throughout, and I had no symptoms of asthma at all. This seems silly to anyone without asthma, but even in my case, I would have been wheezing by the end of the first mile. The next day, I tried again, this time I went further, a little over 3 miles! No symptoms, nothing; I imagine that

that is how anyone else might feel after an aerobic activity, just a little heavier and quicker breathing.

What is more amazing about this is that I have come into contact with the pet bedding that gave me the most severe reaction. I did not want to push it, so I kept the contact minimal, and I have not had a reaction at all. I have had contact with it a few more times with the same results, none!

ERIC B.
Rochester, Minnesota

We are living in an age in which we have the means to directly reprogram the subconscious software and change our lives. Just like bugs in the software on our computers can cause problems with the programs we run, the bugs in our subconscious software will cause problems in our lives. My first experience with the power of subconscious reprogramming was with Theta Healing, where fixing bugs in my subconscious software allowed my frozen arm to heal in an instant!

Let us extend the computer metaphor and talk about what happens when there is a bug in your internal software. Say that you have a favorite Web site for recipes, and you go there and you want to print out a soup recipe to make for dinner. But when you click 'Print', instead of printing the soup recipe, the computer beeps and displays an error message. The "wrong thing" is happening; the computer should be printing your recipe, not displaying an error. Why does this happen? Most likely it is because there is a bug in the computer's software. What can you do about this bug? That depends on who you are and what resources you have access to. If you are a typical computer user, probably the only thing you can do is look for new software updates, or call tech support or your computer repair person and hope that someone else will fix the problem for you. You might try using a different Web browser program, and hope that it does not have the same bug. But if you do not have the ability or the resources to directly work with the software, you simply cannot fix the bug yourself.

On the other hand, if you are a professional software developer and you work for the company that makes the Web browser software and happen to be an engineer assigned to the Web browser project, you may be able to fix this bug quickly and easily. If you have access to the source code for the software, and you have access to the tools used to build the software, and you understand how to debug the software, then you can just go fix the bug. After debugging, the software will be fixed, and you will be able to print your recipes.

Luck Is Simply Our Subconscious Programs

Everything in our lives – health, wealth, relationships, moods, etc. – is created by our subconscious programming. We have software in our subconscious that creates the conditions of our lives, and sometimes bugs in our software cause our lives to do the wrong thing.

Let's say you start a business and you work really hard. But instead of being successful and earning a lot of money, the wrong things keep happening – "bad luck" – and you end up going out of business. Why? Because of bugs in your subconscious software!

There is a saying that "We make our own luck." In fact, our luck really is made *from us*; more specifically, our luck is made out of our subconscious programs.

For example, maybe you are holding a subconscious program that says *"I must be poor to be close to God."* (If you think you might be holding this program, go muscle test yourself and find out!) As a result, it will likely be difficult for you to make money – you will encounter "bad luck" – because you believe subconsciously that to do so would take you away from God. And since you do not want that to happen, it will not! Instead, you will have runs of *bad luck*, and no matter what you do or how hard you work, you just will not seem to be able to accumulate any wealth.

At first it may not seem obvious how failure with a business is like software bugs that prevent you from printing recipes. But they are very much the same thing. In both cases, there are hidden codes creating the problem. And, if you are able to identify the codes and adjust them, it can be a simple matter to solve the problem once and for all. But if you do not know about the codes underlying a problem, or cannot change these codes, then the problem may seem insurmountable!

Theta Healing to the Rescue

How do we access and reprogram the subconscious mind? As with computer software, before we can fix the bugs, we need access to the source code for the software, and the proper software tools used to build the program. Fortunately for us, these things come built in with our human body! We all carry the source code inside of us as our DNA and our subconscious mind's "software", and muscle testing is the primary tool we use to check to see what software we are running. All you need is a tool that allows you to make direct changes to this software, so that you can fix the bugs in your internal software, and your life will change.

Theta Healing is a direct and precise way that uses conscious theta brainwaves to identify and release bugs in our subconscious software so that our lives can change, sometimes in an instant. It is not the only way to do this, but in my experience, it is by far the fastest, most precise, and most thorough method of reprogramming the subconscious mind. The proof is in the results, as you will experience miraculous and wonderful transformations in your life.

Just as with computer software, Theta Healing uses two main methods to fix bugs in the subconscious: certain processes and techniques are used to identify bugs in the subconscious mind, and other processes and techniques are used to fix the bugs.

How to Identify Bugs in Subconscious Software

In order to fix a bug in the subconscious mind, you must first identify the section of code containing the bug. We will call this the "problem program."

If you are having trouble being successful and making money in your life, you might have a problem program such as *"I have to be poor to be close to God"* or *"Money is the root of all evil."* Or, it might simply be that you do not know how to keep the money that you earn, or maybe even that you are afraid of losing all your money – so you try not to have any money at all in order to avoid the risk of losing it. Or you might have all of the above problem programs. Whatever the bugs may be, they must be identified before they can be fixed.

To use a relationship example, you might be holding the program *"Love always hurts."* If you are holding this program in your subconscious, then you will tend to manifest life experiences where you get hurt when you are in love. In order to make a permanent, lasting change in your love experiences, you need to fix this bug in your subconscious software.

Of course, fixing real-life problems in real people is usually not as simple as identifying and changing a single problem program. Just as most bugs in software requires many changes to the underlying source code to completely fix the bugs, there are usually many inter-related problem programs in the subconscious that need to be addressed before your life can change.

The primary way that we identify subconscious bugs is simply by talking about the problems in our lives. It is surprising how often people have an intuitive sense of what the source of the problem is. For example, someone may know inside that they are not angry with their neighbors simply because their neighbors have noisy fights, but rather because their neighbors are triggering memories of their parents having noisy fights when they were a child.

The process of healing often begins by talking about the problem. For example, a woman who develops cancer shortly after she has lost her husband may feel that she is being punished for living longer than he did. If this is the case, that programming must be isolated and changed or she will likely not live much longer. Or perhaps an entrepreneur has started many businesses over the past decade, but was never able to follow through on them to become successful, and he knows that, despite all the striving, he is afraid of success. Therefore, he subconsciously sabotages all his hard work and efforts so that his companies always end up failing. "Bad luck", indeed!

Once you have an idea of what the problem programs are, muscle testing can then be used to determine if you are indeed on the right track to finding the core of the problem. This hypothetical business owner might muscle test TRUE to *"I fear success"*, and if so he had better get rid of that fear of success in his subconscious or he will not be able to create lasting success in his life, no matter how hard he works!

Using Theta Healing to Work with Subconscious Software

Once you have identified the bugs in your software that are causing a problem in your life, with the right techniques you can make quick changes in these codes so that the problem disappears. To do so, we must directly access the subconscious mind.

We do this by achieving a conscious theta brainwave, which opens the subconscious mind and makes it available to direct modification. Because our life experiences effect our subconscious minds the most when we are in a strong theta brainwave, using a technique like Theta Healing to achieve a conscious theta brainwave is a powerful way to directly access and change the problem programs.

Much as a computer programmer knows many algorithms and tricks to work with computers, a well-trained Theta Healing practitioner has a variety of techniques to directly work with the subconscious and fix the bugs that cause problems in our lives. Sometimes these techniques are surprisingly simple, but no less powerful for their simplicity. For example, if the only reason that you are having trouble making money is that you believe you must be poor to be close to God, simply installing new subconscious software to enable you to be rich and close to God at the same time can transform your life and bring you great wealth.

Theta Healing is a Powerful Tool

This book intentionally avoids giving all the exact commands and processes involved in doing Theta Healing. This is because Theta Healing is such a powerful and transformative technique that it would be irresponsible to learn it only by reading a book. (It would be kind of like trying to learn Karate by reading a book – it just doesn't work and is potentially dangerous.) For this reason there is a 3-day training seminar designed to teach you how to use this technique safely and effectively; please see Appendix C or visit the Web site *www.Theta HealingLA.com.*

However, I do want to give you something you can start using immediately, so I have included below the instructions for accessing a conscious theta brainwave, copied with permission from Vianna Stibal's book *Theta Healing*:

Imagine energy coming up through the bottom of your feet from the center of the Earth and going up out of the top of your head as a beautiful ball of light. You are in this ball of light. Take time to notice what color it is. Now imagine going up above the Universe. Now imagine going into the Light above the Universe, it is a big beautiful Light. Imagine going up through that Light, and you'll see another bright Light, and another, and another, in fact there are many bright Lights. Keep going. Between the Lights there is a little bit of dark Light, but this is just a layer before the next Light, so keep going. Finally there is a great, big bright Light. Go through it. When you go through it, you're going to see energy, a jell-o-like substance; that has all the colors of the rainbow in it. When you go into it you see that it changes colors. This is the Laws. You will see all kinds of shapes and colors. In the distance, there is a white iridescent Light; it is a white-blue color, like a pearl. Head for that Light. Avoid the deep blue, blue light because this is the Law of Magnetism. As you get closer, you may see a mist of a pink color. Keep going until you see it. This is the Law of Compassion, and it'll push you into the special place. You will see that the pearlescent light is the shape of a rectangle, like a window. This window is really the opening to the Seventh Plane. Now go through it. Go deep within it. See a deep, whitish glow go through your body. Feel it go through your body. It feels light, but it has essence. You can feel it going through you; it's as if you can no longer feel the separation between your own body and the energy. You become "All That Is." Don't worry. Your body will not disappear. It will become perfect and healthy. Remember there is just energy here, not people or things. So if you see people, go higher. It is from this place, that the "Creator of All That Is" can do healings that will heal instantly and that you can create in all aspects of your life.

A Sample Theta Healing Session

To give a clearer idea of exactly how this works, below is an example of a short Theta Healing session. The Practitioner guides the client through a series of questions and muscle tests to identify the problem programs underlying the life problems the client is having. Once these defective programs are identified, they are transformed with Theta Healing until the muscle tests show that they are gone. At that point the client is ready to heal, and the practitioner facilitates the healing.

In this example, the client has a bad cold, and the healing practitioner is helping to identify the bugs in the subconscious software that are creating the cold. Once these bugs are fixed, the cold can be healed in an instant!

Practitioner: *"How can I help you today?"*

Client: *"I have a bad cold...can you help me?"*

Practitioner: *"Sure... why don't we start by doing some muscle testing?"*

The practitioner leads the client through muscle testing exercises until YES reads strong and NO reads weak.

Practitioner: *"So, why do you think that you got this cold?"*

Client: *"I don't know."*

Practitioner: *"Please muscle test ' I need to be sick.'"*

Client: *"Yes, it is TRUE (strong)"*

Practitioner: *"This tells us that there is some reason your subconscious has decided to make you sick. What is happening as a result of you having a cold?"*

Client: *"I am staying home from work."*

Practitioner: *"Is staying home from work something you only do when you are sick?"*

Client: *"Yeah."*

Practitioner: *"Now we are onto something here...check* 'I have to be sick to get rest.'"

Client: *"Yes, it is TRUE."*

Practitioner: *"I thought so; please muscle test* ' I know how to get rest without being sick.'"

Client: *"No, FALSE."*

This is the core of the problem: the client's subconscious mind only knows how to get rest for the body by getting sick. So, the practitioner just needs to install new software to get rest without being sick!

Practitioner: *"Do you want to learn how to get rest without being sick?"*

Client: *"Yes"*

The practitioner uses the Theta Healing technique to install into the client's subconscious mind new "software" so it knows how to get rest without being sick.

Practitioner: *"Okay, muscle test again – ' I know how to get rest without being sick.'"*

Client: *"It is TRUE now."*

Practitioner: *"Great – now retest ' I have to be sick to get rest.'"*

Client: *"Wow, it is FALSE now."*

Practitioner: *"Perfect. Let's heal it!"*

The healing practitioner has helped the client to release the blocks that prevented the client from healing the illness; the client is now ready to heal. The practitioner now facilitates a physical healing so that the client can hopefully quickly (perhaps instantly!) heal from the cold.

Healing really can happen this fast! One time I had a client with a bad cold with a stuffy head and running nose. After a quick 5 minute session like this, he told me that his symptoms started to clear up even before the healing was finished!

If this seems too good to be true, it is only because you have not experienced it yet. It really can be this easy and this fast, and you really can heal in an instant.

Do you think that your illness or problem is too difficult to be healed in an instant? There is an abundance of evidence to the contrary, as people have instantly healed from a wide variety of even the most serious ailments, including cancer, HIV, autism, and other grave illnesses. Truly, miracles abound!

So what is the secret?

The secret to all healing is that we are creating our own illness out of the programs inside of us.

And once you realize that we are the source of our own problems, an incredible corollary presents itself:

If we are in fact creating our own problems, then we all have the power to solve those problems!

Theta Healing is an incredibly effective, precise and fast way to make this happen. The underlying mechanics of how the Universe really works are fascinating and exhilarating: we really are powerful creative beings!

"Bugs" and the "Fix-It" Metaphor

I have used the metaphor of computer software being like the subconscious mind in order to explain and demystify phenomena such as healing and manifestation. We use the terms "bug" and "fix" throughout. While this makes for clear explanations, these terms imply that there is something wrong with the person who has these "bugs." Of course, we are all divine beings who are perfect exactly as we are; there is truly nothing ever wrong with us, and nobody ever needs to be "fixed." But, if there is something in your life that you'd like to change, then it useful to visualize a "bug" in your software that is causing the problem.

Chapter 7: What exactly is science?

"Within half an hour of the session ending I would noticed that my fever had broken."

I first heard about Theta through Brent about nine months ago, when he offered to help me out with the flu, but my most recent use for his service came a little over a month ago.

I had been ill for a couple of days with what seemed like flu at first. It made me very tired and I did not feel like eating or drinking much. I am guessing that because of lack of fluids I became a little dehydrated and in turn developed a urinary tract infection. This is quite uncommon in men but I had the symptoms.

When I mentioned to Brent that I was ill he asked if I would like to try some Theta for it, and, after discussing my problem over the phone he recommended we start with some muscle testing. Within half an hour of the session ending I would noticed that my fever had broken, though for about two hours some of the other symptoms became more intense, which worried me enough to go see my doctor the following morning.

After discussing the symptoms with the doctor and eliminating things such as kidney stones and sexually transmitted infections, he put it down a UTI, as I had suspected. I was given a quick test for this and he seemed surprised and puzzled when the test was negative but he sent the sample to the lab for a more accurate test. I returned to the doctors a few days later for the results, although I was already feeling much better by this point. Again the results were negative, and within couple more days I was back to normal.

LEE H.

Leicester, England

Before getting into a discussion of the scientific theories underlying healing and miracles, it is important to understand exactly what we mean by "science." In particular, what is the difference between things that are scientific and things that are not scientific?

We typically assume it is easy to determine between what is scientific and what is not scientific. However, these conclusions are often based in erroneous assumptions.

Many people assume that to be *scientific* requires high technology. While it is true that things that are highly technological must be scientific, the reverse is not necessarily true. **To be scientific it is not necessary to involve sophisticated technology!**

Another common assumption is that things that are scientific are always extremely logical. It is true that things that are based upon scientific principles often demonstrate an adherence to logic, and that when broken down into little pieces – analyzed – they will all "make sense" and follow logic.

However, **things do not necessarily need to be logical to be scientific!** Not only are many of the greatest advances in science based upon theories that seem at first to be illogical, but the greatest blocks to these successful but non-logical scientific theories being widely accepted has been that they seem illogical. They therefore are initially rejected as being unscientific only because they are illogical. A perfect example of this is quantum physics. Quantum physics is a highly successful science, yet it is not intuitive or logical.

The Truth about Science

If science is not marked by sophistication or technology or even by logic, then what exactly does it mean to be scientific? In short, to be scientific means to follow the scientific method of accumulating "facts" upon which to base future predictions. The scientific method can be summarized as follows:

1. Create a theory.
2. Make a hypothesis (if the theory is correct, the hypothesis will correctly predict results of an experiment based on the theory.)
3. Design an experiment to test the hypothesis.
4. Run the experiment and collect the results.
5. Compare the results to the hypothesis. If the results match the hypothesis, the theory is successful. If not, return to step #1 with a new theory.

For example, to determine scientifically how gravity operates upon objects of different sizes, we might perform the following steps:

Theory: *"The speed at which an object falls is the same regardless of the mass of the object."* This is our theory, or a proposed understanding of how the world works. We are not sure yet if it is correct, but we think it may be, and we are using the scientific method to determine whether or not our theory is correct.

Hypothesis: *"That a large stone and a small stone dropped from the top of a tall tower will fall at the same rate."* To test our theory, we have designed a hypothesis which makes a prediction as to the result of a particular action, based upon the theory. In this case, our theory is that the mass of an object does not change how quickly it falls. If our theory is correct, then when two stones (one large and heavy, one small and light) are simultaneously dropped from a tall tower, they will strike the ground at the same time.

Experiment: We take two stones, a large stone and a small stone, and go to the top of the Tower of Pisa. We then drop the stones at the same time, and see which one hits the ground first.

Collect Results: When we run this experiment, we find that the two stones do indeed hit the ground at exactly the same time! We run the experiment several times, but each time the results are identical: the two stones hit the ground at the same time.

Compare Results to the Hypothesis: In this case, the results of the experiment exactly matched our hypothesis. We then have established proof that the theory is correct!

You may have recognized this example as a famous experiment in history. Galileo proposed this exact theory, and then made his hypothesis that two stones of different sizes dropped from the same place should hit the ground at the same time. He went and performed this experiment, and found that the results verified this theory, and proved scientifically that all objects fall at the same rate, no matter what their mass is.

Was there anything technological about this experiment? Not at all! Dropping stones is about as primitive and as simple as one can get. (Of course, it is true that some degree of technology is required to build the tower, but the experiment would work equally well dropping stones from a natural cliff.)

But this process *is* scientific. After performing this experiment, we can know with some certainty that gravity affects all objects equally. You might call this scientific knowledge, because it is knowledge based on evidence gathered with the scientific method.

Another important aspect of scientific knowledge is that the experiment it is based on must be reproducible. If different people in different locations cannot perform the same experiment and get the same measurable results, then this knowledge cannot be relied upon or qualified as scientifically valid.

It may seem obvious to us today, but in Galileo's time, many people thought he was crazy for proposing such a theory. Everybody "just knew" that larger, heavier objects would fall faster than lighter, smaller objects; it had to be true because it seemed so logical. But they were wrong, and Galileo was right!

Science Is Not Always Perfect

You may be saying to yourself that while this theory is true in general, there are factors that would cause two objects to fall at different rates. For example, a 200 pound ball of lead and a 200 pound person with a parachute may weigh the same, but fall at very different rates. Even though knowledge gained via the scientific method is generally reliable, it is far from perfect.

Often scientific knowledge is "correct", but incomplete. To extend our example of objects falling, it is true that gravity affects all objects equally, no matter how much they weigh. However, there are other factors that will cause them to fall at different rates, and our theory does not take these into account. For example, a bundle of feathers and a tiny ball of lead may weigh the same amount, but fall at very different rates. Our simple experiment above ignores the density of an object and aerodynamics, as our experiment only measures whether the mass of an object changes how fast it falls. So, while it is true that our experiment predicts that gravity works such that all objects fall at the same rate regardless of their mass, it is still incomplete, as the theory says nothing about other factors that will change the rate at which objects fall.

Scientific knowledge can be seen as the sum total accumulation of all of the theories that are backed by reproducible experiments. As more experiments are done and more evidence is gathered, then the state of scientific knowledge improves and becomes more and more accurate. This does not mean that science always has the right answer, or that scientifically derived knowledge is always perfect or useful. However, it does mean that scientific knowledge is probably your best bet (if you're looking for some firm ground).

We thus believe in scientific theories because when these theories are tested in experiments, the results consistently match what the hypothesis predicted. Of course, scientific knowledge is always evolving and expanding as people do new experiments, get new results and refine their hypotheses and theories.

After doing our simple experiment with objects falling from a tower, we can then expand upon the knowledge gained from this first experiment by creating more theories and hypotheses, and doing more experiments. For example, we might create a new theory that says that the rate at which an object falls is also determined by how aerodynamic it is. We might next create new experiments to test this hypothesis that certain shapes are more aerodynamic than others and cause an object to fall faster. After making many such theories, hypotheses and experiments, we will have a very precise understanding of exactly what causes objects to fall at different speeds. This is how scientific knowledge evolves.

Another Example: Newton's Laws

Before we can start saying whether or not something like healing is indeed scientific, it is useful to examine the real history of science on Earth. Not only is this story educational and entertaining, but it also shows how science is sometimes neither logical nor technological.

A common way in which scientific knowledge advances is when a newer theory refines an older theory to make it more complete, meaning that it successfully predicts the results of experiments in more general and varied circumstances. This does not make the old theory "wrong", as much as it shows that it was incomplete.

For example, Sir Isaac Newton revolutionized the world of science when he published his theories of physics in the 17th century. He proposed three basic "Laws of Motion":

1. An object in motion will stay in motion unless an external force is applied to it.

2. A force F applied to an object with mass M will result in the object accelerating at a rate A, according to the famous equation F (force) = M*A (mass multiplied by acceleration.)

3. Every action has an equal and opposite reaction.

Newton's theories were highly accurate, and seemed to make amazingly accurate predictions of all the mechanical phenomena that people could test and measure. For three centuries, everybody considered his theories to be perfect.

These theories were considered perfect because Newton's Laws always produced hypotheses that exactly matched the results of thousands of experiments over hundreds of years. For example, say you did an experiment and determined how much force F was required to move a certain mass M at a certain rate of acceleration A. The theories of Newton would predict that if you wished to move twice as much mass (2*M) at the same rate of acceleration, you would have to apply twice as much force (2*F). Experiment after experiment proved that "F=MA" was correct.

For example, say that a train is moving 100 miles per hour, and travels for one hour. How far does it go? Well, 100 miles of course! This is Newtonian mechanics, and it is logical, clear, and intuitive. It "makes sense!" One of the great advantages of Newton's laws is that they are intuitive, meaning that they just make sense to us. And they are also logical! After hundreds of years of experiments where every single experiment showed that Newton's equations were correct, most of us would consider this sufficient evidence to believe that the theories were indeed "perfect" and that there were no flaws in them.

As a result, Newton's Laws went unchallenged for a long time, because they seemed to describe everything so perfectly. Scientific knowledge had been gained and applied successfully! But was it perfect? *No.* But it took several centuries for humans to develop the technology to perform experiments that found the flaws in Newton's Laws.

Einstein and Relativity

In the early 20th century, Albert Einstein figured out that there were situations in which Newton's theories did not work. In particular, Newton's theories of gravity did not make accurate predictions about objects that were very large or moving near the speed of light.

We will gloss over the details here, and focus on the simple fact that, given the equation F=M*A, if you have a certain mass M being moved by a force F, then if you double the mass (2*M), you need to double the force (2*F) to maintain the same rate of acceleration. In other words, if a certain force applied to a 10 pound weight makes it accelerate at a certain rate, then you need to double the force to make a 20 pound weight accelerate at the same rate. This "makes sense" and has been supported by many experiments.

However, these results are only true for masses moving at speeds that are very small compared to the speed of light. Because all the objects humans can manipulate on the Earth's surface are moving very slowly compared to the speed of light, it does seem to us that Newton's equation F=MA is perfectly correct. You can run thousands of experiments, and each time the results will support Newton's Laws.

But, if you take an object that is moving really, really super fast (say, 50% of the speed of light), then the equation F=M*A is no longer true! Why? The details are not important, but the short answer is that at relativistic speeds – such as 50% of the speed of light – time actually slows down and objects get heavier, so F=M*A no longer holds.

Why had nobody noticed this for 300 years? Well, because nobody knew how to do experiments to measure what happens when objects move at speeds near the speed of light! It was impossible to show that Newton's theories were incomplete because of the practical limits on experiments.

Einstein was the first to realize this, and he proposed his Theory of Relativity. Relativity builds upon the theories of Newton, but expands and refines them so that they are more accurate in more situations. In particular, Einstein's theories remain accurate even when objects are moving at or near the speed of light.

To prove his theories, Einstein also developed and ran experiments (many involving astronomical phenomena) to provide the tangible proof that his theory of relativity was indeed correct. When the results of the experiments agreed with his hypotheses, his theory of relativity had been proven and new scientific knowledge was gained!

Why does this matter? For one, this is a perfect example of the way that scientific knowledge has progressed. New scientific theories often do not so much replace old theories or prove them wrong as much as they expand and refine the previous theories.

For another, Newton's mechanics are extremely intuitive and logical, and seem very "scientific." By contrast, Einstein's Theory of Relativity is not intuitive and defies common sense. It does not seem natural to think that as something moves very fast, time starts to slow down and the object gets a lot heavier. And in fact, many of the great scientific minds of the time resisted the Theory of Relativity at first because it did not seem logical. But the experiments proved that the Theory of Relativity was correct anyway.

Lastly, the Theory of Relativity has nothing to do with advanced technology. It is simply a statement about the true nature of time and space. While it is necessary to have access to some advanced astronomical technology in order to perform experiments to prove the theory, the Theory of Relativity itself does not require any sort of technological sophistication to understand.

What Science Is, and What Science Is Not

Science is NOT:

- Science is NOT always logical
- Science is NOT always technological
- Science is NOT always correct or perfect

On the other hand, science IS:

- Always growing and expanding as new theories are created and experiments are performed.
- Slowly but surely building upon experimental evidence to create greater and more accurate understandings over time.
- Often the best way to accomplish a goal and discover "truth."

Now that we have established some parameters for talking about what is scientific and what is not, we can revisit the question about whether or not healing is scientific.

To be scientific means to be based on information gathered from the scientific method. The quality of scientific information is based upon the quality of the experiments run from which this evidence is gathered. Thus, there is "good science" and "bad science."

"Good science" means that experiments are tightly controlled, so that the results of the experiment are meaningful. One of the most difficult aspects of learning to work in science is being able to understand the many different parameters that will affect the results of an experiment. In particular, it is very easy to jump to conclusions and assume causal connections for results when there are none.

For example, say that you have a theory that people who drink a lot of orange juice are less likely to get sick. It's a nice theory, and one way to test it is to give a hundred people a glass of orange juice every day for six months, and see how many of them get sick.

Is this a scientific experiment? Yes, in the sense that it conforms to the scientific method. However, it is "bad science" because it does not tightly control for all the different factors that may cause the results to be different. In this case, whether or not someone drinks a glass of orange juice every day is not going to be the only factor that determines whether or not they get sick. Other factors are involved such as what other foods they eat, the kind of work they do, how much rest they are getting, their age, what stresses they are under, where they live, and what other sick people they may be exposed to during the six months. If one of the participants in your experiment is a grade school teacher who is frequently exposed to sick children, that person is more likely to get sick (no matter how much OJ he drinks) than an author who lives and works at home alone. "Good science" controls for all the important factors that can influence the result of an experiment; "bad science" does not.

When I was in college, and later graduate school, one of things that impressed me most was how extremely difficult it is to find truly meaningful "good science" results in experiments. In any real world situation, there are so many factors involved that it is quite difficult – and often very expensive and time-consuming – to create carefully crafted experiments that will control for these factors and produce good results. Early during my first program of scientific research (when I was working on my Bachelor's Thesis at MIT in the area of computer speech recognition under Dr. Victor Zue), I would often run into my advisor's office all excited about the results of one of my experiments. I would say "This is the result, and it means X and Y and Z!" My advisor would calmly correct me and say "No, Brent, it does not, because you did not account for factors A, B, and C." I would return to my desk humbled, to perform more experiments under tighter controls.

Returning to our orange juice experiment, if we take 100 people at random and have them drink orange juice every day, we probably will not get very meaningful results because there are so many other important factors also influencing their health besides drinking orange juice. If we wish to do a better experiment, the first thing we should do is have a control group of people who do not drink any orange juice for six months. This way we can see if there is a difference between a group that drank the orange juice and a group that did not drink the orange juice. We would also want to control for the kinds of things the people ate and drank. For example, you might ask the participants in the experiment to keep a food diary so that you know what they are eating. You might also only allow people into the experiment who eat a particular way, and/or who have a particular job, and/or who live in a particular area, and/or who are of a particular age, and/or who are already in good health.

In the extreme, if you were able to get 200 identical twins who have identical jobs and identical hobbies and identical lives, except for the fact that half of them will be drinking orange juice during the experiment and half of them will not, you would get excellent and reliable and reproducible results. In other words, great science! Why? Because by controlling for all the other factors, any results you get are directly correlated to the drinking of the orange juice. But in the real world, it is never possible to perfectly control for all the variables in an experiment. Usually, the best we can do is put a lot of time, effort, and expense into making our experiments as close to perfect as possible.

Is Healing Scientific?

At the time of the writing of this book (2005-2008), it is probably most correct to refer to healing in general (and Theta Healing in particular) as being in a state of becoming increasingly scientific, but currently based upon bad science.

Why? There are definitely healing practitioners in the world who apply the scientific method to their own healing work, and I am one of those. And I have formed hypotheses based on my theories of how Theta Healing works, and performed experiments and received results that support those hypotheses.

And I can definitely say that other people have been able to perform the same experiments and receive similar results, moving us closer to reliable "good science" experiments with reproducible results.

I always question everything anybody tells me about healing or metaphysics until I have seen some proof for myself. If someone claims that meditating for 9 hours a day for a year will let you walk through walls, I want to see somebody walk through a wall before I am going to devote that much time to meditating! And I certainly am not going to run out and tell all my friends that if you meditate for 9 hours a day for a year you can walk through walls, at least until I have been able to do it myself.

Additionally, there are scientific theories that healing work is based on. While having a theory does not in itself make something scientific, it is a prerequisite for eventual acceptance into the scientific community. Once there is a firm theory established, experiments may be designed that will validate the theory and allow it to be accepted by a larger audience. In the following chapters of this book, I will go into some degree of detail to explain the scientific theories that explain not only how, but also why, a technique like Theta Healing works.

To my knowledge, there have not yet been large-scale efforts to perform "good science" experiments to validate Theta Healing or other similar modalities. This is not because these modalities are not real, or because scientists and healers are too lazy to conduct experiments. Instead, it is primarily because it is incredibly expensive and time-consuming to create "good science" experiments that tightly control for all the available factors necessary to produce "good science" results.

Anybody who has ever been involved in real scientific research knows that science can often take a long time and researchers often need to put in an incredible amount of effort and money towards scientifically proving something that may seem glaringly obvious. But that this is exactly why the difference between good science and bad science is so important! If something just seems to be true, and everybody accepts it is true because it seems obvious, then it is unlikely that anybody would do the difficult, time-consuming, and expensive experiments to prove once and for all whether or not a theory is correct. Fortunately, Galileo did not accept what "everybody knew" – that more massive objects fell faster than less massive objects – and through the scientific method he proved that in fact objects of different masses all fall at the same rate.

In the modern world, a relatively small number of large companies and government-sponsored universities are the primary producers of most of our scientific research. As much as I would love to organize and perform scientific experiments for the healing and spiritual community, the simple fact is that this community does not have or has not yet dedicated the resources to make this a practical goal.

This does not mean that the healing is any less valuable or any less effective. Indeed, gravity did not change in any way when Galileo did his experiments! Instead, it was simply man's understanding of gravity that evolved. To provide a high degree of scientific proof and rigor for healing will require a much larger investment than has been made to date.

Yet the question remains: is healing scientific? Yes, it can be! So far, the theories underlying healing have not yet been supported by a sufficient amount of "good science." But that is okay, because many scientific theories were considered "right" for a long time and were extremely useful to many people before they were scientifically proven correct!

So, just because spiritual healing is not yet "good science" does not make it any less valuable. It simply means that we do not have the ability to present firm scientific proof. By presenting a cohesive theory about the nature of healing, this book is a critical step to bringing healing and miracles into the realm of "good science."

Chapter 8: The Equations behind the Miracles

"My allergic response was so severe, I would have to leave a cat home within minutes... [now I am] among cats without a single symptom!"

I had an extreme cat allergy for over a decade. My allergic response was so severe, (including outrageous sneezing, burning eyes and congestion), I would have to leave a cat home within minutes. After a Theta Healing with Brent, I found myself at a friend's 3-cat home, and had forgotten to take the Claritin in my purse for FOUR HOURS! It was not until I realized I had forgotten to take the Claritin, that I looked at the clock and realized I had would been there so long among the cats without a single symptom! I was comfortable and clear as a bell. This was a fantastic and wonderful lifestyle altering change for me; since I could only spend time at certain homes and functions medicated. No more!

Thanks Brent!

KAY C.
Santa Monica, California

- -

This chapter is devoted to explaining the scientific theories that underlie our ability to create miraculous instant healings and other life transformations by working with the subconscious mind. However, it is not necessary to understand this material in order to benefit from a technique like Theta Healing, or even to be a skilled practitioner of Theta Healing. So, if you are not interested in the details of the science, or become confused by it, it is recommended that you skip ahead to the next chapter, as nothing later in this book requires that you read or understand the material presented in this chapter.

The content presented here is designed to provide you with a theoretical understanding of exactly how known and proven scientific theories interact to allow us to use the conscious theta brainwave to shift the reality around us, and to create magic and miracles in our everyday lives. And after you have taken the training seminar and learned how to perform the Theta Healing technique, you will find this book to be a valuable reference in assisting and supporting your healing work and personal transformation.

Up until now, I have intentionally spoken in abstract terms about how Theta Healing can be used to make direct and powerful shifts in our lives. Later, I will present more detailed accounts of my own personal experiences and those of my friends, my clients, and my students so you can see exactly how "fixing the subconscious bugs" has worked miracles in the health, prosperity, relationships, and spirituality of many different kinds of people.

The True Nature of Reality

To explain how things such as the instant healings are not only possible but actually practical, it is necessary to delve deep into the true nature of the reality we live in. In order to explain miracles, let us start by turning conventional thinking inside out.

The "real world" indeed seems very "real." There seem to be a lot of very real, very solid things out there, such as tables, books, chairs, cars, houses, and mountains. And it seems that innumerable kinds of real events – such as weather or human activity – are happening all the time, all over the world. Based on what we see, hear, feel, taste, and smell, it seems like there is a real, external world that we exist in, that affects us in many ways.

But, instead of thinking of ourselves as mostly helpless beings running around in some external world, being influenced by powerful events and influences outside of ourselves, physicists have come to understand that we are actually more like computers running a sophisticated hologram, sort of like the Holo-Deck (a holographic virtual reality simulator) on *Star Trek*. In fact, they've found that the "external" world does not really exist at all! In fact, it **only** exists in our minds. The 'real world' is really just patterns of energy, and that energy responds to our thoughts and expectations – as proved by many quantum experiments. These energy particles, the true 'real word', are capable of things like being in the same place at the same time, of disappearing and reappearing somewhere else, and other tiny miracles. The 'real world' we perceive – of a big, slow, unmoving mountain for example – is just the result of our limited senses and the brain's desire to put things together into spaces, objects, and nouns that we can label and classify.

For most of us living in human bodies, we experience the world as being full of things that are different, or separate, from us. Of course, the environment around us seems very real. For example, if it is hot out we get warm and start to sweat; if it is cold out we get cold and start to shiver. If someone tells us something nice, we smile and feel good... and if somebody tells us something cruel, we frown and feel bad.

It really does seem that there is an external environment – the "out there" – that affects us. And it does not seem to us that we are creating this environment. Instead, it just seems like we are living in the external world, and that is often much bigger and more powerful than we are.

In particular, it seems that the external world – the "out there" – exists separately from us, no matter what we are doing. It seems to have its own momentum, and it seems very real: the "out there" is full of other people, and animals, and planets, and stars, and companies and governments that seem to be completely separate from us and largely beyond our control.

For example, the Moon seems to be a very real, solid, external object that is "out there." It orbits around the Earth, and whether or not we are looking at the moon, it continues to circle the Earth in its predictable orbit. No matter what we think or believe about the Moon, it just orbits and orbits and orbits, consistently.

So how can it be that there is no moon "out there?" Can it really be true that we are simply creating it with our own minds? The short answer is **yes!**

The documentary movie *What the Bleep Do We Know* has a great line which sums up this truth:

There is no 'out there' out there!

Instead, the external world – the "out there" – is merely a projection of our own minds, based on the codes in our subconscious software. At first this seems incredibly bizarre, because it defies our conventional thinking and day-to-day experiences.

This concept sounds like something that has come out of religion or philosophy. Instead, it has been presented to us by the science of physics. Hence, it is not just a convenient metaphysical concept, but rather a fundamental scientific principal of the Universe resulting from hard science, mathematics, and decades of scientific experimentation.

How did this happen? How did physics and mathematics lead us to an understanding of the Universe that tells us that nothing is actually real, but rather just a hallucination of our own minds?

We will start by discussing conventional Newtonian physics, which describe the mathematical properties of how objects move. These conventional physics make sense to us because they are in alignment with the idea that there is a powerful external world full of "real" objects. In other words, that there is an "out there" out there. Over centuries, further scientific research found flaws in these conventional theories, leading to the 20th century advances we know as the Theory of Relativity and Quantum Physics. It is these modern scientific theories of Relativity and Quantum Physics that tell us that there is no "out there" out there, and that everything in the Universe truly is nothing more than a projection of our own minds.

Newtonian Physics and the "Billiard Ball" Universe

Our intuitive understanding of the nature of the Universe is well described by what is known as Newtonian physics. During the 17th century, Sir Isaac Newton developed a new form of mathematics known as calculus, along with a set of equations –

"Newton's Laws" – that describe in mathematical terms how objects in motion behave.

Newton's First Law says that any object that is in motion tends to stay in motion, unless an external force is applied to it. This is known as the Law of Inertia. It makes sense intuitively: if you roll a bowling ball down a bowling alley, the bowling ball continues to roll until some external force (such as the bowling pins or the gutter) is applied to it and changes its direction.

Newton's Second Law was mentioned earlier; and to refresh our memory, Newton's Second Law is that the relationship between an object's mass (M), the force applied to it (F), and the object's rate of acceleration (A) is defined by the equation $F = M*A$. Thus, if you applied twice as much force to an object, it will accelerate twice as fast. Or, if you apply the same amount of force to an object that is twice as heavy, it accelerates at half the rate. This too is intuitive.

Newton's Third Law is that for every action there is an equal and opposite reaction. We can experience this Law in action when we are in a boat and step out of the boat onto the shore. As we step away from the boat, it tends to move in the opposite direction of where we are stepping. Like Newton's other laws, this "makes sense" to us.

For several centuries, these laws seemed perfect, and many experiments reinforced and confirmed our notion that we live in the external environment where things happen and have momentum. For example, it seems silly to think that the Moon might stop going around the Earth just because we are not looking at it or thinking about it!

According to Newton's Laws, the Moon is an object that has a certain mass and is moving in a certain direction with a certain velocity, all described by mathematical equations. So of course the position of the Moon does not depend on who is looking at it, or what we think about it, but instead is simply a matter of mathematics and gravity. Given the incredible success of Newton's Laws, scientists began to believe that we live in what is called a "billiard ball Universe." Let us say that you are playing a game of billiards, or pool, and say that there are two balls on the table. If you know the position of the two balls, and the direction and speed that they are moving, and their weight, and the amount of friction between the balls and the table and the air, then it is possible to use Newton's Laws and mathematics to determine where both balls will move and where they will stop. Of course, it does not seem to us that the positions of the billiard balls depend on who is looking at them, or what we think about them. Instead, the position of the balls is described only by mathematical equations that include factors such as their position, direction, speed, weight, and friction.

If the Universe is truly like a game of pool, and if the "billiard ball model" is correct, then, if we know the location and the direction that every object in Universe is moving, it is possible (with a lot of complex mathematics) to determine the future of everything in the Universe!

For example, if you know where all the planets are, and the direction and speed in which they are moving, and you understand the mathematics of orbits and the physics of gravity, it is theoretically possible to determine where the planets will be at any point in the future and to determine where they were at any point in the past. And we can more or less do this today; there are software programs available where you can plug in any date in the past or future, and the software will tell you exactly where the planets were or will be at that time.

This poses a dilemma for us as spiritualists because the billiard ball Universe takes away free will. If we do live in a billiard ball Universe, then the future is already set in stone. The Fates seem to have won, and free will is vanquished.

In the arena of healing, spirituality, and metaphysics, whether or not we live in this sort of billiard ball Universe is actually incredibly important. If things in the Universe are like billiard balls – that is, solid objects with mass and momentum and other physical properties that always obey consistent laws of physics – then the future position of these objects depends only on mathematical equations and physical factors such as mass, speed, and velocity.

Let us discuss a real-life example where this becomes relevant. Say that a person is diagnosed with cancer, and MRI scans reveal that they have a large tumor in their body. If we think that the tumor is a real and solid object, then if the MRI scan shows the tumor is there on Monday, we expect that the tumor will still be there on Tuesday and Wednesday. Why? Newton's Laws state that an object that is in motion tends to stay in motion, unless an external force is applied to it. In this example, a tumor that is in the body tends to stay in the body, unless an external force is applied to it (typically surgery, chemotherapy, and/or radiation.) It does not make sense to us that someone can have a large tumor in their body one day, and the tumor can be gone the next day without any sort of an external force been applied to it. Not only does this violate our intuition and common sense, it is a violation of Newton's Laws.

However, many people – in particular Vianna Stibal – have experienced miraculous instant healings from Theta Healing (and other techniques) where tumors literally vaporized and were gone from the body in an instant.

If we actually do live in a billiard ball Universe, instant healings should not be possible. The mathematical equations of Newton's Laws tell us that if you happen to have a tumor in your body one day, it is necessary to have some external force applied to it for the tumor to be gone the next day. But we know from much accumulated anecdotal evidence that many instant healings have occurred, defying conventional explanation.

If you are the kind of person who is extremely skeptical of talk of healings, psychic phenomena, or miracles, a lot of your skepticism is likely rooted in this paradigm of the billiard ball Universe. This is not necessarily a bad thing, as there is an incredible amount of validating evidence supporting the billiard ball Universe theory! It does not make intuitive sense to us that it is possible to heal a cancerous tumor in an instant, to heal a frozen arm without touching it, or that someone who has had asthma for their whole life can have it disappear after a single conversation over the telephone. These things seem impossible because they do not fit within our understanding of the true nature of reality. Yet I have witnessed all of these things occur and know that they are real.

Even the most hard-core skeptics among us must admit that there are an amazing number of miraculous occurrences in the world. Miracles are happening all the time in defiance of scientific understanding. For example, though doctors and scientists understand the way that a fetus grows and develops in the womb, we have no idea what drives and guides the process; even with all of our modern scientific knowledge it is truly a miracle. And many doctors report experiences with patients where they were inexplicably healed of an "incurable" disease. I have personally witnessed hundreds of miracles, all of them events that defy conventional scientific explanation. In the healing community we have a saying – "I do not just believe in miracles – I rely on them!"

How can these miracles happen? Well, it turns out that we do **not** live in a billiard ball Universe! Instead, we are truly creating the entire external world from our own minds. And this is not metaphysics or religion; it is hard science and mathematics.

Introducing Quantum Physics

During the late 19th century and in the early 20th century, science progressed to the point where we were able to begin to learn about the nature of the atom, the underlying building block from which all things in nature are made. Up to this point, the classical equations of Newton's Laws and the billiard ball Universe seemed to work flawlessly.

However, when science began examining the internal structure of the atom, it was found that Newton's Laws were no longer accurate or reliable! Many of us learned in school the "solar system" model for the atom, where we envision the atom as a nucleus of protons and neutrons surrounded by orbiting electrons, much as the Sun in the center of the solar system is orbited by the planets. We expected that, since the electrons and protons and neutrons are all objects that have a measurable mass, the electrons would move around the atomic nucleus as governed by Newton's Laws, much as the planets move around the Sun governed by Newton's Laws. But, this is not what happens!

During the early 20th century, physicists discovered a whole range of contradictory results from experiments with subatomic particles and light. In fact it turned out that the world is much stranger than anyone ever imagined. The higher truth is that there is no "out there" out there, and we really do create the entire "external" world out of our own minds.

The Uncertainty Principle

A brilliant German scientist named Werner Heisenberg published a revolutionary new theory in 1927 called the Uncertainty Principle. It states that, when measuring the position and momentum of a particle, the more precisely the position of a particle is known, the less well known its momentum is. Conversely, the more precisely the momentum of a particle is known, the less well known its position is. Thus, it is not possible to know both the exact position and momentum of a particle at the same time!

Yes, this is really true, and it is a law of physics. You cannot know the exact position and momentum of a particle – any particle – at the same time.

The Uncertainty Principle can be expressed mathematically as the following equation:

$$dp * dx \geq C$$

In this equation, **dp** = the uncertainty in the position of the particle, **dx** = the uncertainty in the momentum of the particle, and **C** = a constant, made up by dividing a number known as **Planck's Constant** by 2 times **Pi**.

Hence, if you know the position of a particle with high precision (**dp** is a small value), then the momentum of the particle must be uncertain and cannot be measured with precision (**dx** must be a large value.) Similarly, if you know the momentum of a particle with high precision (**dx** is a small value), then the position of the particle must be uncertain and cannot be measured with precision (**dp** must be a large value.)

This principle has profound implications for both science and philosophy. For one, it invalidates Newton's Third Law for very small objects. Why? If we actually live in a billiard ball Universe, it would be possible to precisely measure both the position and the momentum of a particle at any given time. If you could accurately measure both the position and momentum at the same time, according to Newton's Laws you could predict exactly where that particle would be in the future! But the Uncertainty Principle tells us that it is impossible to do this. The Uncertainty Principle also tells us that it is not ever possible to determine the precise future position and momentum of a particle, because it is never possible to accurately measure its precise current position and momentum!

At first glance, the Uncertainty Principle does not "make sense" and is not intuitive. How can it be that it is not possible to accurately measure both the position and momentum of a particle at the same time? If we place a billiard ball on a pool table, why is it that we cannot go and measure exactly where the ball is and where it is going? We might place a billiard ball so that it is exactly 2 inches from the bottom left corner of a pool table, and so that it is not moving at all. Doesn't this violate the Uncertainty Principle?

In fact, it does not, because of the size and scale of the objects we are working with. In other words, the Uncertainty Principle is irrelevant when working with objects on a human size scale we are familiar with, such as billiard balls and pool tables and human bodies. However, it is quite important for extremely small subatomic particles.

To understand this better, let us explore exactly what happens when you measure where that billiard ball is sitting on the pool table. First, we place the ball on the table, and get our tape measure. We then measure how far the ball is from the bottom left corner of the table. We see from the tape measure that it is 2 inches away, and so we record our measurement. We have measured both the position and momentum of an object at the same time. Hence, we seem to have defeated the Uncertainty Principle!

But what **really** happens when we take this measurement? Why is it that we think we know where the billiard ball is?

What is really happening when we measure the position of the ball is that light from the room is bouncing off the ball, and then proceeding to hit our eyes, where our brains form the image of the billiard ball in our mind. Because the ball is a seemingly large and solid object, whether or not we have a light on in the room does not seem to influence the position of the ball. For example, we can sit there in the room with the pool table and turn a light on and off all day long, and the ball will not move. Why is this? Because the ball is large enough that when light particles, known as photons, strike the ball, the ball is so many zillions of times larger than the photons that shining light on the ball does not move it.

This "makes sense" to us. Large, solid objects do not seem to be moved or affected by shining light on them. It also makes sense to us that, without the light, we cannot see the ball and hence cannot measure the position of the billiard ball. In other words, we must observe the ball to know where it is, but since the act of observing the ball does not affect it, we seem to violate the Uncertainty Principle.

Now let us imagine that we take the room with the pool table and shrink it down to the size of a subatomic particle, millions and millions of times smaller than anything we experience in everyday human reality. We still need to shine light on the ball to know where it is. However, now that we are the size of subatomic particles, a single photon is as large and heavy as the billiard ball itself. Hence, when we shine light on the ball, the ball will be moved around by the photons that are hitting it!

Thus, in order to measure the ball's position, we must shine light on it. But, when we shine light the ball, it moves. Hence the Uncertainty Principle: you cannot measure precisely the position and momentum of a particle, because every time you shine light on it so that you can measure where the particle is, the light itself moves the particle from the energy imparted to it by the light!

Of course, in our everyday world, shining a light on billiard balls does not move them across the table. In fact, I think that most people would laugh at me for trying to push a billiard ball across the table by shining a light on it. But in the world of subatomic particles, the particles and objects are so small and weightless that they are in fact moved by being hit by even a single photon of light.

In summary, the Uncertainty Principle is real, and in fact at the subatomic level we cannot measure the position or momentum of a particle without influencing it. In other words, when we want to know where a subatomic particle is, the act of viewing its position disturb it... and when it is disturbed, it is no longer where it was before. Wow!

Why Do Newton's Laws Seem to Work So Well?

If the Uncertainty Principle is indeed correct, why is it that Newton's Laws seem to work so well? The answer is that in the world of human experience, everything we interact with is so much larger and heavier than a photon that it seems that shining light on something does not move or otherwise affect it. On the other hand, in the quantum world, the particles are so small that even shining a single photon of light on a subatomic particle will move it in a random direction.

Hence, in the world of quantum physics, probabilities replace certainties.

For example, say that I am the equator, driving north at 100 meters per second. I expect that after one second, I will be exactly 100 meters north of the equator. This "makes sense", and is governed and described by Newton's Laws. We also seem to be cheating the Uncertainty Principle, because by saying that I started at the equator and then moved north exactly 100 meters in the next second, we know both my exact position and momentum precisely at the same time.

But, in the quantum world, things are different. If instead I am in a car that is the size of an electron, I will not be able to say with certainty that I will be 100 meters north of the equator after one second, because I will not be able to measure my position and momentum precisely enough at the same time. Why? Because I must shine a light on my car to know that it is indeed at the equator when I start moving north. However, the light photons are so big and powerful relative to the electron-sized car that the car will be moved in a random direction when the light hits it. Hence, uncertainty!

Although we cannot determine exactly where the car will be one second later, it is possible to use the equations of quantum physics to determine the probability of where it will be. Thus, if I am close to the equator and moving north at roughly 100 meters per second, it will be highly likely that I will be roughly 100 meters north of the equator one second later. In fact, it is likely with an extremely high level of certainty.

However, it is **not** 100% certain, because of the Uncertainty Principle. It is never possible to know exactly where a particle will be in the future, because it is never possible to measure exactly where it is now without disturbing it and moving it somewhere else. So, truly, anything can happen!

So why does it seem that, every time I throw a tennis ball in the air, it falls back down to ground, in a way predictably governed by the Law of Gravity? It is because the outcome predicted by Newton's Laws is the most likely outcome, and at the level of human experience the probability of an object moving through a wall or suddenly teleporting is almost zero. In other words, it is really easy for an electron or other very small particle to teleport or suddenly move through a "solid" barrier, but it is nearly impossible for a tennis ball to do so. But it is not impossible!

In fact, there are stories about a physics professor at the University of California Irvine who would finish every physics lecture by throwing his eraser at the chalkboard, because he told his students that there was a very small probability that the eraser would pass straight through the chalkboard!

It is not important to understand the details of any of the mathematics of the Uncertainty Principle or quantum mechanics in order to experience miracles in your life. However, it is important to recognize that science provides us with the foundation upon which miracles can be built. Indeed, quantum physics has shown us that the fundamental nature of reality is that truly anything can happen.

An Example of Uncertainty

In a billiard ball Universe, the position and movement of a billiard ball depends only upon its initial position, its initial movement, and any force applied to it, as described by Newton's Laws of Motion. For example, if a billiard ball is sitting motionless in the middle of a pool table, then Newton's Laws of Motion tell us that the ball will still be sitting motionless in the middle of the table a moment later, unless some external force is applied to it.

But, if we are in a quantum world where the billiard ball is very small (say, the size of an electron), just because the ball is sitting motionless in the middle of the table at one point in time, and just because no external force is applied to it, does not necessarily mean it will still be sitting motionless in the middle of the table a moment later. It is true that the ball is highly likely to still be sitting there motionless in the middle of the table, but it is not going to be there with 100% certainty, due to the Uncertainty Principle.

So, if the billiard ball is only likely to be sitting there in the middle of the table with some probability, what actually determines where the ball is? The answer is startling: **it depends on who is looking at it!**

Do not be surprised if this seems very strange. Most people have to be exposed to this concept several times before they "get it". And even to those of us who have spent many years studying it, it never really makes much sense.

Let us review this concept with the help of a concrete example. We are going to make a graph, but please do not be intimidated, as I promise that there will be no complicated mathematics involved here.

Say that we have a table that is 9 feet square. Let's draw a graph on this table, and label one dimension X and the other dimension Y, so that each position on the table can be marked as (X, Y) coordinates.

The middle of the table is position (0, 0) on the graph. The first number of the coordinate is the X coordinate (or position on the horizontal axis), and the second number is the Y coordinate (or position on the vertical axis). The middle of the graph is position (0, 0) because both the X (horizontal) and Y (vertical) coordinates are 0 at the center of the graph.

The upper left corner of the table is therefore at position (-4, -4) because the leftmost coordinate on the X axis is -4 and the topmost coordinate on the Y axis is -4.

Similarly, the upper right corner of the table is position (4, -4), the lower left corner of the table is position (4, -4), and the lower right corner of the table is position (4, 4).

We start with the ball sitting in the middle of the table, at position (0, 0), at time T=0. According to Newtonian physics, unless some external force is applied to the ball, the ball will continue to be in the middle of the table, at position (0, 0), forever. And, given the initial position of the ball, and given all the external forces ever applied to it, it is possible to use Newton's Laws and mathematics to determine exactly where the ball will be at any point in the future.

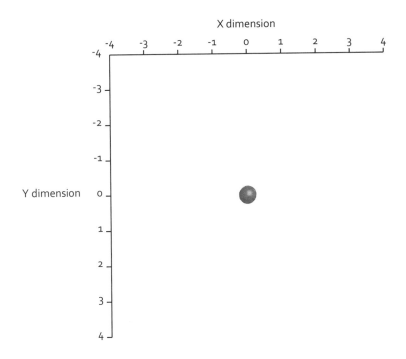

However, what if the table and ball are really, really, super small, the size of subatomic particles, where the size of the table is measured in microns instead of feet? Then, according to quantum mechanics, it is not certain that the ball will always be sitting in the middle of the table, even if no external forces are ever applied to it! This is because of our friend the Uncertainty Principle.

For example, if we know that the ball is sitting in the middle of the table at 1:00PM exactly, then quantum mechanics tells us it is extremely likely that the ball will still be in the middle of the table at position (0, 0) just after 1:00. However, this is not guaranteed with 100% probability. Due to uncertainty, when we shine light on the ball to see where it is, that light will disrupt the ball and possibly move it. So, if we turn on our flashlight and look at the table at 1:00PM exactly, we will see the ball sitting in the middle of the table. But the energy imparted to the ball by the light may move the ball to a different position, so that we cannot know exactly where the ball is just after 1:00PM.

It seems strange to us, but this really is the physics of how our Universe works. The fact that the ball is sitting in the middle of the table at one point in time only means that it is highly likely to still be there later, but it is not a guarantee. Instead, at just after 1:00, quantum mechanics gives us a probability distribution for where the ball is likely to be. Just because the ball has been affected by light to measure its position does not mean that the ball will have traveled to the opposite end of the Universe; instead, it is highly likely to still be in the center of the table, or very close to the center of the table.

The probability distribution for the ball at slightly after 1:00 might look like this:

Position (0, 0):   90% probability

Position (-1, 0):   1% probability

Position (1, 0):   1% probability

Position (0, 1):   1% probability

Position (0,-1):   1% probability

Position (1,-1):   1% probability

Position (-1,-1):   1% probability

Position (-1,-1):   1% probability

Position (1, 1):   1% probability

All other positions: very small (less than .01%) probability

According to this probability distribution, if the ball is at position (0,0) at 1:00 and is not moving, then just after 1:00 the ball is 90% likely to still be at that same position (0,0)...but it is not guaranteed to be there!

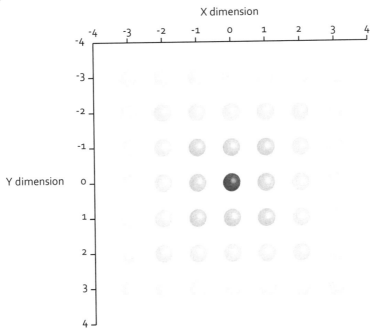

There is also a 1% probability that the ball will have moved to one of the positions very close to the center position. All these positions are close to the center, so there is a small but real chance (in our example, 1% probability) that the ball will be at one of these positions at just after 1:00.

There is also a very small probability that the ball will have moved to one of the other positions far away from the center of the table. However, because we know that the ball was at position (0, 0) at the center of the table at 1:00, there is only a very small probability that the ball will have moved itself to a position far away from the center of the table shortly after 1:00. And there is an almost zero probability that the ball will have been moved to the opposite side of the Universe. (But note that the chance is almost zero – not exactly zero – because anything is possible with a very low probability.)

Quantum physics tells us that the exact position of any particle cannot ever be determined with 100% accuracy. However, we can develop probability distributions that determine where a particle is likely to be based on where it was in the past.

Of course, this begs another important question: if we cannot know the exact position of the ball based only on its previous position and momentum, then what actually determines where it ends up? In other words, when we shine light on the ball to measure its position, what determines which direction the ball moves? For example, if we look at the ball on the table at just after 1:00, what determines whether the ball is still sitting in the middle or whether it has moved to one of the other positions? It depends on who is looking at it!

Schrödinger's Cat

Before we go further in discussion of the Uncertainty Principle and quantum mechanics as they apply to metaphysics and miracles, let me relate a famous thought experiment of quantum physics called **Schrödinger's Cat**.

Erwin Schrödinger was a brilliant physicist in the early 20th century working in Western Europe. There he developed advanced theories and mathematical equations for quantum mechanics to explain the inner workings of the Universe. He also developed a story that helps illustrate one of the important concepts of quantum physics. And since I am an animal lover, I have modified the story to be more animal friendly than the original version.

Let us say that you have a big cardboard box and there is a cat inside the box. You know that when you close the box, the cat is awake. There is also a vial of sleeping gas in the box, attached to a small computer and a small robot. After the box has been closed for one minute, the computer generates a random number. A minute after that, we open the box to check on the cat.

If the computer generates an even number, the computer sends a signal to the robot, which smashes the vial, releasing sleeping gas into the box and putting the cat to sleep. So, when we open the box, we will find a sleeping cat.

But if the computer generates an odd number, it does not send a signal to the robot, and the vial is not smashed. So, when we open the box, we will find the cat to be wide awake.

We will also assume that this cardboard box is perfectly sealed, so that we have no way to determine whether the cat is awake or asleep without opening the box.

So, after two minutes, is the cat awake or asleep? Common sense tells us that the cat must be either awake or asleep. Either the computer generated an even number that caused it to give the signal to the robot to break the glass, or it did not.

But, quantum physics tells us that this is not how it works. Instead, the truth is that the cat is both awake and asleep – with 50% probability of each – until the box is opened. Indeed, until the box is opened, *the cat is both awake and asleep at the same time.* It seems strange, but the quantum physics has proved this.In our example of the billiard ball on the table, we talked about being able to assign a probability distribution to where the ball is likely to be. When we say that the cat has a 50% chance of being awake, and a 50% chance of being asleep, this is the probability distribution for the cat in the box.

Again, this is very strange and not intuitive, but it really is the way the Universe works. Until we open the box, the cat is both awake and asleep at the same time, with a certain probability for both.

Hence, the cat in the cardboard box is both awake and asleep at the same time until somebody opens the box and looks at it. It is only when the cat is observed that one of the probabilities is chosen, and the cat becomes either awake or asleep. When we open the box with the cat, we force the cat to either be awake or asleep.

Returning to the billiard ball example, if we know that a billiard ball is sitting on a pool table – but we do not know exactly where, because we have not looked at it yet – then the ball is actually in every possible position on that table, with varying probabilities. It is only the act of someone looking at the table and measuring where the ball is (which involves shining light on it) that causes one of these probabilities to be chosen and the ball to start actually existing only at one particular position on the table.

Nothing is real until Witnessing Makes It So

We now have the answer to our previous question about what determines whether the billiard ball is still sitting in the middle of the table or has moved to some other location: it depends on who is looking at!

Again, this seems strange and wrong at first, since it does not seem to us that something must be observed in order to make it real. It is common sense that just because we do not look at the Moon at night, it does not mean that it stops being there or that it stops orbiting the Earth, or that the Moon is no longer affecting the tides on Earth with its gravity.

Physicists call the probability distribution a wave function, and the process of observing or measuring something is called "collapsing the wave function." We might view the wave function for the cat in a cardboard box as the following:

Outcome #1 = cat is awake = 50% likely

Outcome #2 = cat is asleep = 50% likely

Until somebody opens the box and actually looks at the cat, the cat exists in both states at once, both awake and asleep, and both with 50% probability. When somebody opens the box and looks at the cat, the Universe must choose which state the cat is in: is it awake, or asleep? Depending on which choice is made, the person who opens the box may see that the cat is awake, or they may see that the vial has been broken, the sleeping gas has been released, and the cat is sleeping.

Before the box is opened, whether the cat is awake or asleep is described by a wave function, which is a probability distribution. But after the cat has been observed, this wave function collapses, and one particular outcome is chosen and witnessed as "real."

The Double Slit Experiment

Another famous experiment of quantum physics explains this concept in more detail. It is known as the "Double Slit" experiment. Originally this experiment was performed in 1805 by an English scientist named Thomas Young. This was a very long time before the development of quantum physics, because this experiment was originally created to answer a question about the nature of light. However, the result of this experiment was so unexpected and so bizarre that it took scientists over a century to develop the scientific theories of quantum physics to understand and describe the results.

Scientists of the 19th Century had two competing theories about the nature of light. One theory was that light is made up of particles, called photons, and that light was actually a stream of particles moving through space. Another theory was that light was a wave, moving through some sort of mysterious substance called the ether, very similar to sound waves or ocean waves. The double slit experiment was developed to determine once and for all whether or not light is really a wave or a particle.

To perform the experiment yourself, start with a light, a cardboard screen, and some photographic film. If you turn on a light and cut holes in the screen, the light comes through the slits in the screen, hits the photographic film, and is recorded as an image.

In the simplest version of this experiment, we turn on the light and cut a single slit in the cardboard screen. As expected, a light comes through the slit and hits the photographic plate. There is a lot of light directly opposite the light source, and the amount of light falls off as we get further away from this point.

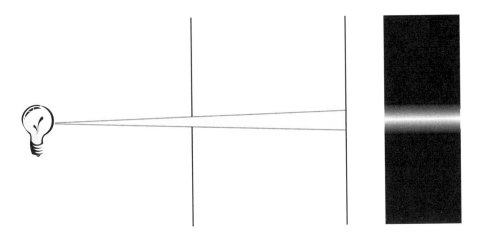

Diagram A: One slit, and one concentrated area of light

This seems to confirm the particle nature of light. It "makes sense" that the light particles move away from the light source, and those that go through the slit accumulate on the photographic plate.

Next, we cut two slits into the cardboard, and turn on the light. Interestingly, in this case the light makes an alternating pattern of light and dark bands on the photographic plate.

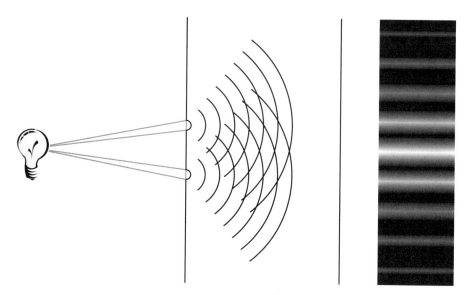

Diagram B: Two slits without photon detectors,
and alternating bands of light and dark

At first glance, this seems to confirm the wave theory of the nature of light. It makes sense that if light is a wave, then the light waves traveling through the two different slits will come through the other side of the cardboard and interfere with each other, creating a pattern of alternating bands of light and dark on the photographic plate. Again, this happens because each light wave passes through *both* slits, and these waves interfere with each other on the other side of the slits.

On the other hand, if light were actually a stream of particles, we would expect that each individual light particle would have to travel through one slit or the other, and so we would expect to have a result on a photographic plate that represents two large points of light, slowly falling off in intensity – looking very much like the light distribution for having a single slit, except that there would be two bright spots, one for each slit.

But just when we thought we had light figured out, quantum mechanics comes and throws a monkey wrench into the whole works! Let us repeat the same experiment with the double slit, but place very sensitive photon detectors by each of the two slits. This ensures that as the light comes through the slits, we know that every photon of light must pass through one slit or the other, and we use photon detectors to measure which slit each photon passes through.

Common sense tells us that placing photon detectors by the slits in the cardboard screen should not make any difference in the pattern of light recorded on the photographic plate. After all, the light will be moving through the slits in exactly the same way, whether or not we have photon detectors, won't it?

The answer is **no, it will not**! As strange as it may seem, it is actually true that the pattern the light forms on the photographic plate depends on whether or not you measure which slit the light photons pass through. Amazing!

If you do not use the photon detectors, and so do not measure which of the slits each photon of light passes through, then light acts like a wave, and causes the alternating pattern of light and dark bands on the photographic plate, as in diagram B. In essence, the light waves move through both slits, and interfere with each other on the other side to create the bands of light and dark.

But if you do use the photon detectors, and you do measure which slit each photon passes through, then light acts like a particle, and causes two bright areas to appear on the photographic plate, as in diagram C.

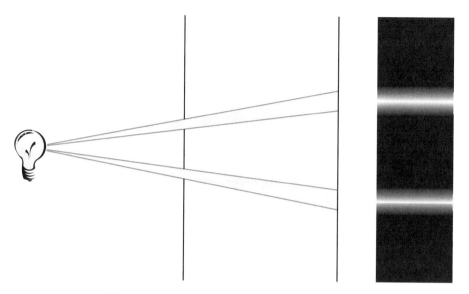

*Diagram C: Two slits with photon detectors, and
two concentrated areas of light*

This defies common sense; it does not make sense that whether or not we measure how the light is coming to the slits should affect the pattern of light in the photographic plate. But it really does!

What is going on here? This is the same effect we were discussing earlier with the examples of the billiard ball and the cat in the cardboard box. If we do not measure which slit the photons are coming through with photon detectors, this is like leaving the box with the cat closed. The light remains a wave function and a probability distribution, and the light wave truly does pass through both slits and interferes with itself on the other side to form the alternating pattern of light and dark bands on the photographic plate.

On the other hand, if we do use photon detectors and measure which slit the photons pass through, then what we are doing is collapsing the wave function of the light when it hits the slit, forcing it to go through one slit or the other. This is analogous to opening the cardboard box and determining whether the cat is awake or asleep: if we are looking at the cat, the cat obviously must be either awake or asleep, and cannot be both at the same time. If we do not measure which slit the light is moving through, then the light actually moves through both slits with varying degrees of probability, and acts like a wave. But if we do measure which slit the light moves through, then the light wave becomes a stream of particles, collapsing the wave function and forcing it to go through one slit or the other.

Weird, but true! Light acts like a wave until we look at it and measure it, and then it acts like a particle. So, light *really is* both a wave and a particle at the same time, depending on how you look at it. The Double Slit experiment proves this. You will see a result that matches either diagram B or diagram C, depending on whether or not you use photon detectors on the slits.

So what exactly happens when the Universe must make a choice and collapse a wave function? One theory of quantum physics postulates that every time the Universe must make a decision like this, the Universe actually splits into two, and both outcomes occur. So, if you opened the box with the cat in it, you would split the Universe in two. In one Universe the cat would be awake, and in the other Universe the cat is asleep. This is known as the Parallel Worlds theory, and has been backed by luminaries of the physics world such as Stephen Hawking.

The Parallel Worlds theory is a real mind-bender, as we are literally creating new Universes just by opening cardboard boxes! But we truly are this powerful, and nothing can actually exist in the Universe without it being witnessed. Until something is witnessed, it exists as every potential all at once, with varying degrees of probability. It is only the act of witnessing that causes the wave function to collapse and one result to be picked to actually exist.

Chapter 9: The Science of Energy Healing

"The pain in my right knee and my lower back could be described as excruciating... after my first Theta session with Brent, I was able to resume my normal work schedule."

I was desperate when I called Brent for my first Theta Healing appt with him (I am a Theta practitioner, and had been working on myself. Note: the core issues around my brother I was totally unable to begin to address). I had fallen on the ice in early January, and had gotten to a place by early Feb. where pain in my right knee and my lower back could be described as "excruciating", pain levels I had not experienced since labor with my children.

By the time I called Brent, I was cancelling appointments for the rest of the week. I was in too much pain to pretend I could be of service. 24 hours after my first Theta session with Brent, I was able to resume my normal work schedule, and the acute pain was at least 50% less. After our second session two weeks later, I enjoyed even greater pain relief. Now, some three weeks after our first session, I still have a bit of weakness in the knee and the lower back is still a bit stiff, yet I feel confident, because day by day there is less pain and more strength and mobility. I should mention in closing that before calling Brent, I had 5 chiropractic adjustments, as well as deep tissue work on the leg and knee area, all of which had no, absolutely no lasting effect.

Thank you, Brent, for allowing me to get back to enjoying my life!

KAREN Z.
Boulder, Colorado

How Real Magic is Possible

The key to creating magic in the real world lies in the equations of quantum physics. Fortunately, like using modern cars or personal computers, we do not need to understand these equations to benefit from them. So, do not worry if the previous discussion of quantum physics did not make sense to you. The more often you are exposed to these concepts, the more sense they will make, and it is not necessary to understand them to apply the *Formula for Miracles* to transform your life.

Quantum physics tells us that truly anything is possible, and just because something is in one place at one time means only that it is likely to still be there in the future. Nothing is certain, and anything can happen!

Let us take an example that is closer to the healing world. Say that a person has a cancerous tumor in their body, and it shows up clearly when they have an MRI scan on Monday. Newtonian physics and the billiard ball Universe would tell us that, unless we apply some external force to the tumor – like a surgery – it will still be there on Tuesday.

But quantum physics tells us that the tumor is only likely to still be there on Tuesday. Indeed, it is possible – though perhaps unlikely – that it will disappear entirely and the person will be healed, without any sort of an external force being applied to it.

From one perspective, Theta Healing can be seen as a technique that adjusts and engineers these probabilities so that we maximize the likelihood of that person no longer having the tumor in their body on Tuesday. Remember, until somebody actually goes and looks at the tumor, it is both there and not there with different degrees of probability. If we are able to use a technique like Theta Healing to influence those probabilities, it may disappear entirely.

Miraculous instant healing, all within the framework of physics!

There is no "Out There" Out There!

The implications of quantum mechanics are profound. For one, we finally have the answer to the question of whether or not a tree that falls in the forest makes a noise if nobody is there to hear it. In fact, the tree both falls and makes a noise, and does not fall and does not make a noise, with some probability, both at the same time. This is the same way that the cat in the cardboard box is both awake and asleep at the same time, at least until we open the box and look at it. Once we open the box, the Universe must make a choice, collapsing the probability wave into a particle.

Once we understand that every possible reality exists in potential, until we actualize or draw it to us it becomes easier to accept so-called miracles. Much as a billiard ball sitting in the middle of the table is only likely to be there with a certain probability a second later, a man standing on water is going to fall through the water with probability that is a tiny bit less than 100%, meaning that there is some probability that the man can stand and walk on the water. If we were somehow able to get the Universe to always choose the probability where we are standing on the water, even if it seems extremely unlikely, then it becomes actually possible to walk on water.

Quantum physics makes impossible things into improbable things. It is not that walking on water is impossible; instead, it is just that walking on water is extremely unlikely. But improbability is a much easier barrier to overcome than impossibility!

The fact that you may not have seen anyone walk on water means that this is not an easy feat. However, I do believe it is well within human capability, and there are stories of people (particularly a famous Rabbi from Nazareth who lived 2000 years ago) who have walked upon water.

How the Universe Chooses a Possibility from Many Options

Given that anything is possible with varying degrees of probability, who or what does this choosing to pick one possibility over another? In the example of the person with a cancerous tumor, what determines whether or not they wake up the next morning after their MRI scan and still have the tumor (x% likely), or wake up completely healed (y% likely)? What causes the Universe to go on the same way, or change? Why do some things happen to us, and not others?

The answer is simple: the programs of our subconscious mind!

Earlier we discussed the nature of the subconscious mind, and how it is the programs in our subconscious mind (the software of our soul) that create all of the experiences in our lives. Now, we can tie this to the above discussion of quantum physics and propose a theory as to how this is all actually working.

I want to emphasize here that this is only a theory. I cannot offer any "good science" studies that provide solid evidence that this theory is correct. However, I can provide a large amount of experiential and anecdotal evidence that fits the theory.

Additionally, the theory seems to be both internally consistent and elegant, both of which are hallmarks of successful and eventually provable theories.

At each new moment in our existence, the subconscious programs inside of us create the illusion of the physical reality around us, according to the codes written in our DNA. Because all humans have extremely similar DNA (human DNA is approximately 99.9% identical), we all experience the illusion of reality to be quite similar. For example, all humans find that gravity affects us the same way.

But as much as each of us is similar, each of us also has a very different experience of life. We all have different DNA, and even those of us that share essentially identical DNA (such as identical twins) still experience life differently. This is because the software of the subconscious consists of more than just the genetic level. It also encompasses the other levels – Core, History, and Soul – including memories imprinted into the subconscious software from other times and places and the impact of our experiences from this lifetime.

The commonality of the human experience – we all tend to want to be fulfilled in our work, enjoy good food, desire good health, long for a loving and compatible partner, etc – tells us that we are far more similar than we are different. But at the same time, we are all unique, and have individual tastes, attitudes, expectations, prejudices, and beliefs about ourselves and the world around us. Remember that the Uncertainty Principle tells us that position and momentum of a particle cannot be measured precisely at the same time. In the example with the billiard ball, if the ball is sitting in the middle of the table and no extra force is acted upon it, it is extremely likely to still be in the middle of the table a moment later, but this is not

100% certain. If we look at the table, there is a very small probability that the ball will be in one of the corners, despite the fact that nobody moved it from the center.

According to the current scientific understanding of quantum physics, when we look at the table, the Universe makes a seemingly random choice and places the ball somewhere when we observe it. Most of the time, the ball will be exactly where it was last seen, but not always. On the surface it appears that the mechanism that chooses the outcome is totally random, governed only by probability. So, if we put the ball in the middle of the table and blink our eyes over and over and look at it trillions of times over billions of years, perhaps only once will the ball have moved into the corner of the table. Nearly every time in those trillions of trials the ball will still be where it was last seen, exactly as determined by Newton's Laws of motion.

But what if this choice was not always random? What if you could actually pick where the ball was going to be when you look at the table? In other words, what if you could actually pick whether Schrödinger's cat was going to be awake or asleep every time you open the cardboard box? If you could do this, you could perform miracles! In fact, a true master, someone who has conscious control over matter and energy, would be able to bypass the so-called Laws of Physics entirely and teleport, moving instantaneously from one location to another. How is this possible?

This is the basis of the phenomena we call "luck." We all know people who are lucky, and people who are unlucky. Some people can gamble on slot machines and tend to win money, despite the fact that the odds are stacked strongly against them, whereas most of us tend to lose money when we gamble on slot machines, according to the Laws of Probability. Is this just a coincidence?

Or is it really possible that some people can bend the Laws of Probability?

What if you could win 60% of the time on slot machines? Or, even better, what if you could bend the "hard" Laws of Physics and walk on water, heal people instantly, teleport across continents, and read thoughts?

Being a "master" simply means that you have the proper subconscious programming that allows you to consciously pick what you experience and create through these quantum choice points, ignoring the effects of mass consciousness and the Laws of Probability. Every time something happens where there are multiple possible outcomes – such as opening the box with Schrödinger's cat in it – the Universe makes a quantum choice and picks one outcome or the other. Most of us experience this as occurring unconsciously, according to Laws of Probability. But in fact, these choices are made according to our subconscious software, and with the proper internal programming, we can actually learn to bend these probabilities and pick the quantum choice that we like the best. Hence, with the proper subconscious software, you can open the box with Schrödinger's cat and find the cat awake 70% or 90% or even 100% of the time, if that is your choice. *You really can*, and this is how miraculous healings work!

Thus, if you are a "master" and you wish to teleport across the room, all you need to do is consciously choose the absurdly unlikely – but not impossible! – possibility that all the particles in your body spontaneously move across the room and reassemble themselves into you again without any extra force being applied. If you have the right software running inside of you, this will work!

Yes, this means that "masters" are able to manipulate probability, and hence manipulate matter and energy. Yes, if you are truly a "master" and have the proper subconscious program, you can go to Las Vegas and gamble and win every single time. (A good example of a scenario representing how a master might do this was an episode of the TV show *Las Vegas* where a Buddhist monk came to the casino and prayed in front of slot machines and won every time.) This is simply good manifesting, which can be taught and practiced with techniques such as Theta Healing.

The Truth about the Laws of Physics

If it is true that we all create our own experience of reality, then why does it seem that there is this consistent, solid, "real" external world? If we all create our own experience of reality, why is it that we all see the moon orbit the Earth according to strict mathematical equations? Why is it that some things simply seem to be true? Why is it that we all measure the gravity on Earth as a force that accelerates falling objects at the same rate (approximately 9.8 meters per second squared?)

Very simply, the most likely quantum probabilities – the ones described by the so-called Laws of physics – are manifestations of mass consciousness. The way it works is that if you do not have a strong program within yourself about the way something is, you will instead take on the programs from the mass consciousness around you. So, unless you have specific programs within yourself that allow you to transcend gravity, you will take on the mass consciousness gravity programming, which we all experience to be identical because we are all sharing the same programs of mass consciousness!

Is it possible for humans to levitate or even fly? I believe that this is definitely within the realm of human potential, and that humans have done this on Earth before and will do this in the future. Do I know how to do this as of the day I am writing this book? Not yet, but I know it is coming, because in order to levitate or fly, we only need to reach the level of mastery over our own internal gravity programming so that our personal subconscious programs take over in place of the mass consciousness programming about gravity. When we are able to do this, then we can bend gravity and levitate!

Quantum Physics Tells us Anything is Possible, and Our Subconscious Programming Determines What is Possible for Each Individual

Science has proven that quantum mechanics is real and provides a proper description of the true nature of our Universe. Many of our modern technologies, including computers and all electronics, are based on these theories, and the fact that computers and stereos work at all is proof that the theories of quantum physics are real and correct, at least within a limited context.

However, like any science, we cannot claim that quantum physics is perfect, and it will likely undergo additional refinement over time; for example, quantum physics is not sufficient to correctly predict the behavior of particles in or near a black hole. However, it seems unlikely that any of its major theorems or understandings will be completely overturned.

Truly, we live in a magical Universe where the scientific theories of quantum physics tell us that anything is possible. Even better, with the techniques of Theta Healing and muscle testing, we have been given the means to identify the subconscious programs that drive how we create our reality by making these quantum choice points, or the decisions we make that influence the quantum reality of things.

When you are exposed to a virus, what determines whether or not you get sick? Your subconscious programming, of course! Because each time you are exposed to a virus, you will both be infected and uninfected with some probability. But if you have the proper subconscious programming, the probability of being infected will be very small, and if you are a "master" you can simply choose to never ever be infected. This is why some people can go into a room full of contagious sick people and stay perfectly healthy, while others may get sick right away.

Similarly, whether or not you continue to have a tumor in your body is determined by your subconscious programming. When Vianna Stibal instantly healed the cancer in her leg, she used visualizations and commands from a theta brainwave state to make a conscious quantum choice to choose the extremely unlikely, but not impossible, outcome that at the next moment in time, her body would re-create itself without cancer. And it worked! In an instant her body was healthy and strong, without cancer. After that, the probabilities were strongly in her favor that her body would continue to keep creating itself without the cancer, so no further healing work was necessary for her to stay cancer-free.

In terms of my experience with my frozen arm, when I had my first Theta session with Terry, we started by clearing the subconscious programming that caused the arm to be frozen. Once that was done, she then performed the physical healing, where visualization and commands from a theta brainwave state helped me to make a quantum choice to re-create my arm the next instant without the elbow being frozen. And it worked: instant miracle healing achieved!

But would any healing have worked to unfreeze my arm before we fixed these "subconscious software bugs" and clear out all the subconscious programs that got in the way? It probably would not have, because the subconscious software inside of me would not have allowed the quantum choice to re-create my body without the frozen elbow. But once I was no longer running subconscious programs saying I needed the frozen arm, my subconscious was ready heal it, opening me to the possibility of a miraculous instant healing. Hence, when Terry used the Theta Healing technique to facilitate a physical healing, my body was recreated in the next instant with a mobile, functioning arm. And it worked!

We have seen how we humans are all little magical creation machines that are constantly manifesting the experience of life around us out of our internal subconscious programs via our DNA. And, like a computer user, if there are bugs in the software that we are running, then we will have problems in our life, such as illness, injury, poverty, loneliness, or pain.

Fortunately, we all come equipped with the source code to the subconscious software that creates our reality, as well as the tools to identify and change the bugs in the software! In particular, we are able to use muscle testing to identify exactly which subconscious programs we are holding that are interfering with our life experience, and we are able to use techniques such as Theta Healing to fix the bugs and change our internal software so that we create a different experience of life. By learning to work with our own subconscious software, we can truly create a life of joy and health and happiness that we have always dreamed about. **You can really do this!**

Now let's have some fun and extend our computer software analogy by adding the Internet. In doing so, we will expand our understanding of mass consciousness, and see what is really happening in terms of the physics and metaphysics when we do things that defy the "laws of physics", such as instant miracle healing. Yes, you really can bend the laws of physics with proper subconscious reprogramming. It is relatively easy to learn to bend time, and it is something that I teach in the Advanced Theta Healing class. Teleportation and walking on water are more extreme examples of miracles, but – at least in this author's opinion – instantly healing a serious physical condition in the body also qualifies as a miracle that defies common sense, even though so-called miracles are supported by the laws of physics.

The Internet

The advent of the Internet – and more importantly, the commercialization of the Internet that occurred in the 1990s – has been one of the most profound and important events in the history of humanity. In addition to all of the amazing things that the Internet has already done for us, it will now play one more role and help us to understand the true nature of reality a little more clearly.

Why have computer networking and the Internet been so amazingly powerful and transformative? In large part, it is because we are able to access the knowledge and experience and resources of many different people through efficient electronic organization. For example, if I want to know how to make a chocolate mousse, all I have to do is type "chocolate mousse recipe" into a search engine, and I will see a thousand different recipes for chocolate mousse. This is incredibly easy to do, because I am able to leverage the experience of millions of other people with chocolate mousse to quickly and easily get a recipe I can use for myself.

One way to understand the changes that are created in the subconscious software by a technique like Theta Healing, is to imagine that we are connecting you to the cosmic Internet, to bring in new software that is not already part of your system.

Why is it possible that we can make such profound changes in people's subconscious software? Well, because we can leverage the experience and intelligence of all humanity via the cosmic Internet that we are all connected to!

Let's say that you have bought a new printer for your computer. If you hook it up and it does not work, you might call your computer maintenance person and he will tell you that you are missing the proper printer driver. (A printer driver is a program that allows the computer to talk to the printer.) Most likely your computer person will come over and download this driver program from the Internet and install it on your computer. Generally this process is very easy and fast, and within 20 minutes or so your printer will be working.

Now, let us say that your computer person did not know about the Internet. Then, he would probably tell you that you have got a serious problem, because you need to get the software that lets the computer talk to the printer. He tells you that you are in luck, because he can write the software, but it will take six months and cost you $50,000!

Theta Healing uses a "cosmic Internet" that has all the intelligence and experience and advice and knowledge from all humans (and possibly other more advanced beings) across all space and time. This is truly a vast storehouse of information and knowledge, so much so that you never really ever have to write your own software from scratch, because you can always find exactly the software you need out there on the cosmic Internet!

Likewise, if you have been wondering if you can ever be any good at this Theta Healing technique because you are not a technical person and could never program your way out of a paper bag, do not despair! You do not actually have to know anything about writing software to be a truly amazing and effective healer. In fact, there are many talented practitioners who know little or nothing about computers or science. Instead, you just need to learn a few tips on how to go find the software you need on the "cosmic Internet" and install it.

If it was necessary for us to write all our new subconscious software from scratch, then using Theta Healing to heal a serious life challenge would be a long and complicated process. But it is not, since we do not have to do it all ourselves from scratch, as all the subconscious software we need is available for download.

And, unlike real computers, we all run the same operating system, and the software you download from the cosmic Internet will never have bugs or viruses or other incompatibilities. Having been a professional software engineer for many years before doing Theta Healing, I can say that reprogramming the subconscious with Theta is about 100 zillion times easier than fixing computer software!

Online Computer Games as a Metaphor for the True Nature of Reality

To further expand the computer metaphor to understand how mass consciousness and the so-called laws of physics fit into the true nature of reality, let us take a moment to talk about one of my personal favorite subjects: online games!

In a traditional computer game, the player buys software in a box at the store and installs it on her personal computer. She then plays the game by herself, and we call this a traditional single player game.

Starting in the 1990s, networked computer games became much more popular. The earliest network games ran over local area networks, where the computers are connected by cables. Then, games started to use the Internet to connect many players separated by vast distances into the same game at the same time. These are called online games.

Online games are actually quite sophisticated and technically challenging to properly design and build. I know this well, because I spent over 10 years running an online game development company called Lyra Studios. The way an online game works is that every player who is playing the game installs onto their individual computer the game client software. They then run the "game client software", which uses the Internet to connect to a central server for the game. The player then "logs into" the game server, and the game server passes communication messages among all the game client programs so that they know where the other players are in the world and what they are doing.

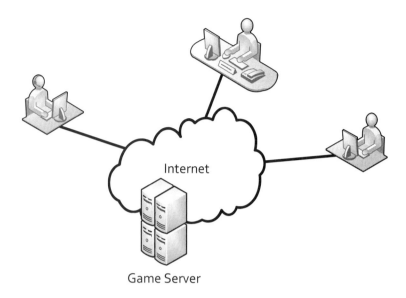

Game Server

The most technologically sophisticated of these games are known as graphical massively multiplayer online role-playing games. In these games, every player's machine runs the game client software, which contains the graphics for the world, and all the instructions, rules, and codes for the game to operate. Each player has an identical copy of the client software.

When you run the game program and log into the game server, your game client software renders a realistic-looking 3D display upon the computer screen. You will see the game world and all of its graphical details, including buildings, trees, underground areas, and anything else the game designers and artists could imagine. You can walk around in the world, and if there are other players "logged in" to the same game at the same time, you will actually see them walking around!

How does this work? The concept is simple, even if the implementation is extremely challenging and sophisticated. The game client software that resides in every player's machine contains all the information about the game that stays the same. This includes all the graphics for the world, the architecture, and the rules for the game. So, when the game is running, all this common information – rules, graphics, architecture, sounds, etc. – does not need to be sent over the Internet. In fact, to do so would be impossible, because this is far more information than you can fit over even a high-speed Internet line.

But when a player starts the game and logs into the central server, the server sends messages to the game client software on each player's machine that tells them where the other players are and what they are doing. If you are alone in a room and another player enters that room, the server will send your computer a message, and your game client software will draw that person on the screen so that you can see them. Similarly, if you are in a room with another player and there is a bench, and you take your sword and smash the bench into little pieces, then a signal will be sent to the server and then onto that other player's client software to tell them that the bench has been smashed, so that it can show the smashed bench on the other player's computer screen.

One thing that is important to note about the way online games work is that they are designed so that every player has the same client software. This is important, because you want all of the players to experience an identical game world. For example, every player should see the same graphics in the same places, every player should see the same monsters, and every player should be playing by the same rules. If a player is somehow able to cheat and alter their game client software, they can change the rules of the game for themselves only. For example, you might make yourself invulnerable to the attacks of all other players and monsters. Game developers put a lot of time and effort into being able to prevent and detect cheaters, because if the game is going to be fair for everyone, then everybody must be running the same client software.

When I was the head of Lyra Studios, I used to enjoy playing our online game called *Underlight*. This game is typical of graphical online role-playing games, and consists of a shared virtual world where players could login and interact with others and the environment. Because I had designed and written much of the game myself, and I was the head of the company that ran the game, I had all of the source code and all the software development tools for the game on my computer. Hence, I was able to cheat and change the game code for my computer's game client software, and do things that were otherwise impossible for all the other players. For example, there were certain magical spells that could not be used in certain areas of the game because the game client software simply prohibited this. However, by changing my client software, I could change the codes that prevented these spells in certain areas, and as a result I was the only person in the game who could cast these spells anywhere in the game world. Hence, I was able to do things that other people thought were impossible, because I was able to access change the underlying software codes.

So, even though everybody else in the game was forced to run the same software, I was able to edit the codes in my game client software to make it do things that seemed impossible for everybody else. Truly, I was an ascended master of *Underlight!*

Reality Works Just Like Online Games

Our individual experiences as humans are very much like people playing in this online game. Each of us comes with our own software on our system, and our client software is very much like everybody else's client software. Hence, we tend to have the similar kinds of experiences with "reality." For example, we all measure gravity to be the same, and Newton's Laws seem to work exactly the same for all of us, because for the most part we are running identical client software in the "game of life."

With Theta Healing, we are able to go in and change our own internal software, so that we can have a different experience of the game of life. At the same time, we are all connected to a cosmic Internet, so all the new software that we need is freely available. If we play the game of life and we do not like what we see, we can simply download some new software from the cosmic Internet and change our life!

The effect of mass consciousness upon our life experience is very much like the game client software that comes with an online game. If you do not do anything to modify the codes of your software, you will have the same game world and same rules as everybody else because you are running exactly the same software. In fact, the online game world will look identical to all the players, so it will simply be accepted as the truth that this is the way the game "just is", and anyone that claims differently will be labeled as crazy.

For example, if you log into an online game and always see a blue monster in the first room, then this monster is like a belief system that has been entrenched in mass consciousness. In other words, it is part of the standard game client software that every player is running, and as a result, every player that enters the game will see a blue monster in the first room.

If you do not know how to change the game client software codes on your computer, then you will always find a blue monster in the first room when you log into the game. In fact, hundreds or thousands of other people will also always find the blue monster in the first room, and this will occur so consistently that everyone will accept it as the truth. And you will probably be labeled crazy or insane if you start telling people that there is not a blue monster in the first room!

The laws of physics and our common experience of reality are very much like this game client software. Mass consciousness runs our lives and provides a similar experience of gravity, health, love, etc., unless we are able to change the codes of our own internal software to create a unique, customized life experience. Having access to Theta Healing is like being the person who wrote the game software and owns the game company; with it we really can edit and configure and customize our own software to have the life we choose!

So, how is it possible to transcend gravity and levitate? It is simply the ability to edit your own programming about gravity in your subconscious to make it work differently for you than it does in mass consciousness. In the game *Underlight*, characters were not able to fly, and there were software codes to create a form of gravity in the world so that characters that walked off the edge of a wall would fall to the ground below. And unless you had access to the game source code and had the right tools and experience, your character would always fall when walking off a ledge, because that is just how the game software was programmed. But, for me, I was able to edit the gravity software for my game client software and turn it off so that it would not affect my character, Lord Xenus. Hence, Lord Xenus was able to fly! Everyone who saw this thought it was impossible, and knew that either I was a cheater, or one of the programmers on the Lyra Studios staff.

Creating miracles and our own experiences as humans is no different than editing the game client software for an online game (though admittedly it is easier said than done.) We simply need to identify the programs inside of us that are causing the bugs or troubles or things we do not enjoy about our game of life experience, and reprogram them so that the game software operates differently.

Now that we have a good understanding of how our subconscious programs create our reality and how we can use the technique of Theta Healing to reprogram ourselves and change our lives, it is valuable to examine the major areas where we encounter bugs in our subconscious software.

I have found that the problems people address with techniques such as Theta Healing fall into roughly 4 different categories. The most common reasons that people turn to Theta Healing are:

- Health Problems
- Money, Wealth, Prosperity
- Relationships
- Spirituality

Chapter 10: Theta Healing for Health Challenges: Illnesses, Injuries, Emotional Problems, Weight Loss, and More

"I had a severe bone infection in my jaw bone from a previous root canal gone bad and once it had been detected by a dentist I immediately got surgery from a holistic clinic. After the surgery, I was still having major problems and I was getting worse, maybe due to the infection that wasn't being detected in the gum and bone area. I was facing more surgery and I didn't want that.

I prayed for a miracle and healing through some sort of energy work. One day I was speaking to a friend and he mentioned Theta Healing which sparked an interest in me, I found out more about it and received a healing from Brent a couple of weeks later. Brent worked on me over the phone and cleared up the infection in the bone in 40 minutes.

Theta Healing really works!"

QUINTELLA T.
Los Angeles, California

Before beginning our discussion of how Theta Healing can help with health problems, note that nothing presented in this book is intended as medical advice, nor is it intended to diagnose, treat, or cure any disease or condition. Theta Healing is a process of focused prayer and meditation to allow a higher power – God,

Source, The Universe, or whatever term you prefer – to intercede and make changes in our lives, including physical and emotional healing. Nothing presented in this book is intended as a replacement or substitute for medical care from a licensed practitioner.

The most common reason people turn to a "voodoo" technique like Theta Healing is because they have a serious health crisis. In fact, many of the serious high-level Theta Healing practitioners (including myself and Vianna Stibal) got involved with this sort of thing because of a serious health problem that defied treatment by Western medicine.

If conventional Western medicine had been able to cure me of my problems, I likely would have gone right back into my software engineering career and lived my life in pretty much exactly the same way I did before my health crisis. Like many people, I spent the first years of my own health crisis seeking a solution only in conventional (allopathic) medicine, spending countless hours in physical therapy and in doctors' offices, and using splints, heat, ice, and drugs. At best, these treatments only took the edge off the pain, and provided no measurable or lasting benefit. In fact, my condition only continued to get worse.

When I first discovered alternative medicine, I thought "At last, something that will work for me!" So I dove headlong into many of the better known and more widely accepted alternative modalities, such as deep tissue massage, chiropractic, and acupuncture. These modalities at least seemed to have some rational basis, and I always avoided the really weird stuff like energy healing until I had run out of other options.

Like many logically-minded people living in the Western world, I trusted science and not "voodoo" to get me better. So, it was only when I was truly at the end of my rope – when I saw no possibility of ever recovering any sort of life worth living – that I swallowed my pride and tried something as crazy as Theta Healing.

I see no shame in this, though of course in retrospect I wish I had opened my mind earlier, as it would have saved me years of fruitless and often painful treatments and well over a hundred thousand dollars in medical expenses.

I also needed an experience as dramatic and in-your-face as a miraculous instant healing on my frozen arm to convince me that this crazy Theta Healing stuff was real. To everyone reading this book who thinks that what you have read so far is interesting, but are unsure if it will work for you, know this: I spent **years** trying everything under the Sun, and nothing worked for me until I tried Theta Healing.

Theta Healing for Physical Illnesses and Injuries

The process of using Theta Healing to heal any sort of physical challenge is as follows:

- First, the client and practitioner work together to perform muscle testing and ensure that they are getting accurate results.
- Next, the client and practitioner discuss the client's problem and use intuitive readings and muscle testing to explore the client's subconscious to identify the hidden codes, programs, beliefs, and traumas that are sponsoring or underlying the health challenge.
- Once the subconscious programs underlying the health challenge are identified, the practitioner then uses the

Theta Healing technique to fix these "bugs" and install new "subconscious software" promoting health.

- Once the subconscious has been reprogrammed to release the illness or injury, a physical healing is performed, where the practitioner uses a conscious theta brainwave to access Source energy and witness the healing.

I have personally witnessed hundreds of instant healings of various physical injuries and illnesses. However, sometimes the healing does not show up instantly, but rather takes overnight or even several days to manifest. Other times, the Theta Healing session does not instantly heal you, but by clearing your subconscious blocks to healing, you soon thereafter manifest other resources into your life that will bring you the result you are seeking. For example, my frozen elbow healed instantly and completely during my first Theta Healing session, but the rest of my problems (tendonitis, carpal tunnel syndrome, depression, back pain, etc.) did not heal instantly. However, after using Theta Healing to clear my subconscious blocks to health, all the other therapies that I had been doing for years without any success – physical therapy, acupuncture, homeopathy, deep tissue massage, etc. – suddenly started delivering results! In my case, Theta Healing was not the only thing I needed, but it was the magical key that unlocked my subconscious blocks and allowed me to start healing. For me, the same treatments from the same people that had done nothing for me prior to Theta Healing magically began to work for me. For those who are familiar with the Law of Attraction, what happens is that once your subconscious is programmed for health, you attract to you the resources that you need to heal completely.

It is important to emphasize that the Theta Healing practitioner is **not the healer!** The practitioner is merely a facilitator of a process that allows the client's body to heal itself. During the physical healing, the practitioner is not healing the client, but instead is witnessing the healing.

An Example of Physical Healing: Cat Allergies

If you have any sort of any sort of problem in your life, including any kind of illness or injury, there are a few basic muscle tests you can perform to determine if there is a subconscious underlying issue that needs to be addressed. For example, if you are allergic to cats, you could check to see if there is an underlying subconscious reason by muscle testing yourself with the statement "I need to be allergic to cats." If the muscle test result is TRUE (or strong), then there is some reason that the allergy is there, and it may be difficult to get rid of the allergy until that reason is addressed.

In a Theta Healing session, the practitioner might ask questions to find the right statements to muscle test to begin the process of debugging your internal software and healing the allergy.

The following is an example of a Theta Healing session to heal a cat allergy:

Practitioner: *"What can I help you with today?"*

Client: *"I am allergic to cats."*

Client sneezes

Practitioner: *"OK, let us start with muscle testing 'I am offended by or allergic to cats'."*

The result is TRUE

Practitioner: *"OK, that is what we expected. Now test* 'I need to be allergic to cats'.*"*

The result is TRUE

Practitioner: "Do you know why you need to be allergic to cats?"

Client: "I have no idea."

The practitioner uses the Theta Healing technique to do an intuitive reading and connect to the cosmic Internet to download the reason why the client is allergic to cats.

Practitioner: *"This may sound a little crazy, but I am getting that the allergy is there because you are holding a traumatic past life memory in your subconscious mind about being killed by a tiger. Please muscle test the statement* 'I am holding trauma from being killed by a tiger'.*"*

The result is TRUE; the practitioner then works with the client to release this trauma from the subconscious. Sometimes a trauma is not anchored by other subconscious programs and releases quickly; other times, there will be multiple underlying reasons why a traumatic subconscious program is held, and it will take more debugging to completely release it.

Practitioner: *"OK, it seems like the trauma has been cleared. Now let us retest the statement* 'I am holding trauma from being killed by a tiger'.*"*

The result is now FALSE

Practitioner: *"Great! Now let us retest* 'I need to be allergic to cats'.*"*

The result is now FALSE. In this example, the cat allergy was anchored only by the trauma of being eaten by a tiger, so clearing the trauma means the allergy is no longer needed by the

subconscious mind. In other cases, it might be that after you have successfully cleared the trauma from being killed by a tiger, you may find that there are other reasons that you believe you need to be allergic to cats. This is evident because the statement *I need to be allergic to cats* is still TRUE. In this case, the practitioner needs to continue to work with you to identify and release all the underlying reasons for needing the cat allergy. When they are all released, you will no longer need the allergy, and it can be quickly and easily healed.

Practitioner: *"Cool... let's heal the allergy, OK?"*

Client: *"Sounds good!"*

The practitioner now uses the Theta Healing technique to witness a physical healing of the body releasing the cat allergy.

Practitioner: *"OK, now let's retest* 'I am offended by or allergic to cats'.*"*

The result is now FALSE

Client: *"Awesome!"*

The client now goes and rubs his face against a cat!

This story of a person being allergic to cats because she has a past life memory of being eaten by a tiger may seem far-fetched, but this example is in fact based on a true story! The first time that my Theta Healing client and later student Bette came to me for a private session, I was working out of a private home with two cats. Because Bette was allergic to cats, within a few minutes she started to react to the cats. Her allergy was so bad that she thought that she might have to leave, but I said "Nonsense, we can heal that!"

So I immediately had her muscle test the statement *"I am offended by or allergic to cats"*, and the result was TRUE. We then muscle tested the statement *"I need to be allergic to cats"*, which also was TRUE. We talked about this a little bit and I did some readings with Theta, and we found that she was holding trauma in her subconscious mind from being killed by a tiger. In Theta Healing terminology, this is a past life memory, or a subconscious program held on the History Level.

We worked on the trauma with Theta and were able to clear out all the "bugs" in her subconscious software that said she needed to be allergic to cats. This took less than 10 minutes. After that, I witnessed the physical healing on the allergy. She immediately stopped reacting to the cats, her eyes and throat cleared up, and she never had a problem with cat allergies again!

Theta Healing for Emotional Problems

"For the last 19 years of my life I suffered terribly from bipolar disorder and after many doctors' visits and many treatments nothing worked. Then [I heard about Brent] and I was very amazed to find out that his frozen arm healed instantly just after one session of Theta Healing and I decided to give Theta Healing a try.

It was the best decision of my life: only after just one session with Brent Phillips my bipolar symptoms are gone and I got a bonus on top of that: I'm now driving the car of my dreams: a $30,000 Lexus! All this within a month!

Theta Healing really works if you believe in it! I highly recommend it!"

TONY D.
Los Angeles, California

The process of using Theta Healing for emotional troubles — whether it is for anger, jealousy, childhood trauma, phobias, or any other sort of emotional dysfunction — is the same as for physical healings:

- First, the client and practitioner work together to perform muscle testing and ensure that they are getting accurate results.
- Next, the client and practitioner talk and use intuitive readings and muscle testing to explore the client's subconscious to identify the hidden codes, programs, beliefs, and traumas that are sponsoring or underlying the emotional problem.
- Once the subconscious programs underlying the emotional difficulty are identified, the practitioner then uses the Theta Healing technique to fix these "bugs" and install new "subconscious software" promoting emotional health.

I've found that I have a high rate of instant healings on clients with emotional troubles. In my personal experience, a majority of clients I work with on emotional issues experience a significant emotional shift in their very first session. This is particularly true for clients who have been affected by traumatic experiences that happened a very long time ago, such as in childhood.

Although deep seated emotional issues and traumas may take several sessions over time to clear completely, it is rare that I have a client who doesn't feel significantly better after even only a single session. When I first started doing Theta sessions with Terry after my elbow surgery, I liked to say "Terry, my problems were far from solved, but I do feel marginally less bad about my life!"

The reason that Theta Healing is so powerful for emotional healing is that our feelings are created, or sponsored, by our subconscious programs. This may seem remarkable at first, because emotions so often defy logic and seem to be mysterious and enigmatic, to the point that emotion is sometimes seen to stand in diametric opposition to logic and reason. However, the process of Theta Healing allows us to quickly and easily reprogram our subconscious software, and immediately feel differently. As an engineer and someone who lived entirely in his head for so many years, learning how to change my feelings with Theta Healing was truly magical, since I finally found a method to apply a methodical, precise process to work with my emotions and actually change how I felt about things.

It is common in Theta Healing sessions to have the client experience intense emotions when discussing old trauma. However, inevitably I am able to quickly and gently guide the client through the process of subconscious reprogramming to fix the defective software causing the sadness, or anger, or guilt, or whatever the negative emotion is. One of my favorite parts of being a healing practitioner is frequently being privileged to witness a client heal and transform from a quaking, crying, nervous wreck into a calm, stable, confident, and joyful person in a matter of minutes; it is truly amazing! And if this seems too good to be true – if you think that profound emotional transformations require months or years of therapy – then you obviously haven't done Theta Healing!

Clearing Fears and Traumas

"On the afternoon of the last [Theta Healing] session I flew to Europe. We had worked on fear of flying and it was totally gone! I was really surprised, that even during some turbulence I was completely calm and felt

none of the usually anxiety. I actually had to calm my boyfriend and tell him that everything was fine...it was really amusing to me... cause I used to be the one who freaks out. "

> **INES B.**
> *Los Angeles, California*

- -

One of the most powerful uses of Theta Healing is to clear fears and traumas out of the subconscious. By doing the proper subconscious reprogramming, it is possible to dramatically and instantly change how we feel about things and release old fears and traumas that are just holding us back.

While the most obvious use of clearing fears is for issues such as phobias, I have found that deep-seated fears and traumas underlie many health problems, both physical and emotional. By clearing these fears and traumas, we are able to free ourselves to live life the way we desire.

I had an experience when I was in college that beautifully illustrates the power of clearing fears in transforming our lives. I grew up in Southern California, so when I arrived at MIT for college, I had never ice skated. But, my girlfriend loved to ice skate, so she insisted on going ice skating on the first night of public skating at the campus ice rink.

However, before we actually started skating, she took me outside and had me practice falling down on a block of ice over and over again, for about 20 minutes. After a while I was getting a little bruised and frustrated, since I was looking forward to an evening of skating, not an evening of falling down on a hard, cold block of ice. But, after she was convinced I could fall down without hurting myself, we went inside and started skating, and in my very first time on ice it only took a few minutes before I was zipping around the rink and having a great time.

By contrast, every other person who was on skates for the first time was standing rigid and holding onto the side rail. Why? Because they were afraid of falling! And what happens when you are trying to ice skate, but are afraid of falling? You get rigid and tense, which not only makes you more likely to fall, but will also make it more likely that you will get hurt if you do fall.

So the moral of the story is: *As long as you are afraid of falling, you cannot learn to ice skate!*

Did I fall that night? Of course I did, but because I was not afraid of falling, I had a great time skating and I did not fall very often. When I did fall, I just got up, brushed myself off, and kept going.

Many of our experiences in life are just like my ice skating experience. So often, it is only our own fears that are holding us back from wonderful things.

To use the Theta Healing technique to clear fears and traumas, we like to play a game called "What is the worst thing that would happen if…" To get at the core of any fear, we need to explore the worst thing that might possibly happen. This game will quickly lead us to the bugs we need to fix in the subconscious in order to release the fear immediately and permanently. An example session is provided below:

Client: "*I am afraid of public speaking. It is terrifying to me to stand in front of a group of people; I get nervous and start shaking and cannot speak.*"

Practitioner: *"This is a common experience. Let us do some muscle testing and check your subconscious by muscle testing the program 'I fear public speaking'."*

The result is TRUE.

Practitioner: *"OK, I am not surprised that you are holding that fear in your subconscious. Please tell me, what is the worst thing that might possibly happen if you spoke in front of a group of people?"*

Client: *"I know this sounds crazy, but I am afraid if I say the wrong thing, I will be attacked and maybe even killed."*

Practitioner: *"OK, let us muscle test that –* 'If I say the wrong thing in front of a group, they will kill me'. *"*

The result is TRUE.

Practitioner: *"I am not surprised – now let us muscle test* 'This happened to me before'. *"*

The result is also TRUE.

Client: *"Wow, I had no idea..."*

Practitioner: *"OK, it looks like you have a fear of public speaking because you are connecting to a genetic or past life memory where you were killed for saying the wrong thing in front of a group. We could do regressions and readings to find out the details, but the drama is not important. Instead, what is important is to clear the trauma out of your subconscious mind. Let us muscle test* 'I am holding trauma from being killed for saying the wrong thing'. *"*

The result is also TRUE; the Practitioner now leads the Client through the process of clearing this trauma until the muscle test for

'*I am holding trauma from being killed for saying the wrong thing*'
yields a FALSE result.

Practitioner: *"OK, now that the trauma is cleared, let us recheck the*
fear. Please muscle test 'I fear public speaking'.*"*

The result is now FALSE.

Client: *"This is incredible; I do not feel the fear at all anymore...wow!"*

By digging down to the core of the fear with the "What is the worst thing that would happen…" game, it is possible to quickly and thoroughly release even fears that have dominated our lives.

Theta Healing for Weight Loss and Healthy Metabolism

Theta Healing can be an incredibly powerful tool to release subconscious blocks and belief systems that prevent us from achieving our ideal weight and body composition. For grammatical simplicity, this section will assume that the client is overweight, but the same process applies to those who are underweight.

Because the need for weight loss and a healthy metabolism is such a common health problem, I have developed a powerful and effective Theta Healing process for healing it. The issues I commonly work on for weight loss are:

- Emotional eating
- Emotional reasons to carry excess body fat
- Food allergies and sensitivities
- Proper nutrition and cleansing

Theta Healing has proven to be powerful in healing issues of emotional eating, which can be roughly defined as all the reasons we eat other than for nutrition. Common reasons for emotional eating include:

- Eating to process stress, grief, sadness, anger, and/or other emotions
- Eating to self-medicate and balance the brain's chemistry
- Eating to stay busy, be entertained, and/or process boredom
- Eating because it is a habit
- Eating because we are actually thirsty but can't tell the difference (this is really common!)
- Eating because we are tired

Fortunately, all of these emotional eating issues can usually be healed quickly and easily with a bit of reprogramming of the subconscious mind with Theta Healing.

Another area where many of us have blocks to weight loss and healthy metabolism involve subconscious beliefs that tell us that it is dangerous to be thin and healthy, or that we don't deserve to be attractive. The most common core issue here is fear of intimacy, and many of us unconsciously eat poorly and carry excess body fat in order to make ourselves less attractive to potential romantic partners and therefore shield ourselves from intimacy. As with emotional eating, clearing the fear of intimacy is usually quick and easy with Theta Healing.

On the physical level, reprogramming the subconscious mind to process and digest food, absorb nutrition, and eliminate food allergies can be extremely powerful in increasing energy, releasing excess weight, and achieving a healthy metabolism and ideal body composition. For most people this can be done extremely quickly, and rarely takes me more than a single session to clear all food allergies with Theta Healing! (Food allergies are cleared in a manner very similar to the example of a cat allergy presented earlier in this chapter.) I saw proof of this when I cleared my wheat, sugar, and dairy food allergies with Theta Healing, and then took an ALCAT panel, which is a blood test sent to a lab to check for about 100 different food allergies. When my results came back, my doctor was shocked that the results reported I had absolutely no reaction to wheat, sugar, or dairy; in fact, he was so surprised that he told me that we must have my blood type wrong, because it was impossible for someone with my blood type (O+) to have no allergy to wheat, sugar or dairy. So he had my blood type tested again, and – no surprise to me – it came back as O+…and after that he signed up for his first session of Theta Healing!

I have also had success using Theta Healing to heal people who are overly sensitive and reactive to certain foods and nutritional supplements.

The last piece to the weight loss, healthy metabolism, and ideal body composition puzzle involves providing the body with proper nutrition and giving it the resources needed to cleanse out toxins and poisons. Due to modern agribusiness farming techniques, our modern food supply – even organic, natural foods – has been badly depleted of essential trace minerals, which is having a profound negative impact on human and animal health. At the same time, processed foods lack the enzymes needed for the proper digestion and assimilation of nutrients and the elimination of toxins from the body. Compounding this effect is the toxicity of the air, water, and food in our modern world, causing us to build up unhealthy levels of various poisons and toxins in the body (including but not limited to heavy metals such as mercury, aluminum, and arsenic, and poisonous chemicals such as insecticides on plants and antibiotics and hormones in food animals.)

Once the proper subconscious clearing has been done on all the issues listed above, some people will naturally shed excess fat and arrive at their ideal metabolism and body composition, but others may require some additional physical support. I have had amazing results, both personally and with my friends, family, and clients, with a nutritional cleansing program that provides the body with both the missing nutrition and the cleansing resources needed to feed the body properly and cleanse out harmful toxins and poisons.

I believe I have now finally "cracked the code" to weight loss and healthy metabolism with a combination of Theta Healing and nutritional cleansing, and there is so much to say about this topic that I've written an entire book on the subject – *Spiritual Weight Loss*, released in 2009. (You can get more information on *Spiritual Weight Loss* online at www.ThetaHealingLA.com)

Taking the Next Step: Healing Your Body and Mind

This book is designed to give you a deep and thorough understanding of how healing works as well as a roadmap to how you can transform your life. When you are ready to actually start clearing your subconscious blocks, there are four resources available to apply Theta Healing to clear your subconscious and heal your own physical, emotional, and weight problems:

- Theta Healing private healing sessions
- Theta Healing group healing sessions
- Theta Healing block clearing audio programs
- Theta Healing training seminars

Theta Healing private sessions with professionals like me are probably the most powerful way to heal as fast as possible...and maybe I will soon add **your** testimonial about your miraculous instant healing to my Web site!

I also have specially designed audio programs that will use special technology combined with Theta Healing to actually clear your blocks while you listen to them! I call this the *Formula for Miracles*™ technology, and it is discussed in further detail in Appendix A.

Additionally, I regularly offer group healing tele-seminars available through my Web site and through my *Formula for Miracles VIP Club*. The VIP Club is designed as your #1 online resource for applying Theta Healing to your life to see real results right away, and includes access to all my live group healing tele-seminars, access to recorded tele-seminars, discounts on all private sessions, as well as private forums that I answer daily and many other benefits, available at a price everyone can afford. (More information about the VIP Club is presented in Appendix B.)

Over the long term, you will gain the most benefit from learning to do Theta Healing yourself by attending a 3-day Basics of Theta Healing seminar. I teach these seminars on a regular basis in Los Angeles, and am available to travel if you would like to host a seminar in your area.

There is a saying that *If you give a man a fish, you feed him for a day...but if you teach a man to fish, you feed him for life.* Theta Healing private sessions are like being given a fish, whereas taking the training seminar and learning to do Theta Healing for yourself is like learning to fish...or, in this case, learning a profoundly powerful healing technique you can use to heal yourself and your friends, family, and pets for the rest of your life!

I've made it my personal goal that, by December 21, 2012, I will teach at least one thousand people how to do Theta Healing, and I want those thousand people to go forth and each teach another thousand people how to do Theta Healing. Working one on one, we can solve the problems in our individual lives...but I know that thousands or millions of us working together can tackle the "big picture" problems in our world, including but not limited to violence, crime, war, theft, starvation, disease, political instability, global warming, corruption, and pollution.

If you'd like to join me on this journey, you can find more information on the Basics of Theta Healing seminar in Appendix C.

Chapter 11: Theta Healing for Money, Wealth, and Prosperity

"I have been a traveler on the spiritual path for the past thirty-five years and have been quite successful at manifesting things, situations, and experiences, but they seemed to come haphazardly and I would never know when the sought-after what-ever might show up. In spite of my dedicated, systematic effort, chance seemed to maintain its control over my stated intentions. Something always seemed to be missing from my creation process. And then I was introduced to Brent Philips and Theta Healing. Less than a week after the two-and-half-day, Theta Healing training ended, I manifested a much-needed reliable automobile that with some repairs is now worth about $4,000. Two weeks later, a 1990 Toyota Camry in excellent condition and low mileage was given to my wife. My personal relationship with Connie has changed dramatically for the better. I can already notice a significant improvement in my physical health. My state of being has shifted from fear and self doubt to self-confidence and peace of mind. For the first time ever, I feel like I am in charge of my life. The Theta Healing training has been one of the best things I ever manifested.

Thank you, Brent. Thank you, Vianna. Thank you, Theta Healing."

ROBERT C.
Winnetka, California

After health challenges, the second most common reason people come to me for Theta Healing is for prosperity. Many of us – including myself – have struggled with money problems, even though we may be "good" people who work hard and "do the right thing." Healing people to bring prosperity in their lives is extremely important to me, since I see poverty as being the single most prevalent and single most dangerous disease that exists on Earth today.

Is it possible that a technique like Theta Healing can not only heal us physically, but also help us to make more money and enjoy a life of abundance and prosperity? At first, this may not seem likely, because we think of healing as being a purely physical or emotional thing. However, remember that every aspect of our life – every little tiny bit of it – is created out of our subconscious programs. This includes the level of wealth and prosperity that we enjoy!

Many of our highly successful self-help gurus – everybody from Napoleon Hill (*Think and Grow Rich*) to Joseph Murphy (*Think Yourself Rich*) to T. Harv Eker (*Secrets of the Millionaire Mind*) – have been telling us the exact same thing for decades:

The level of wealth and prosperity that you enjoy in your life is not about how hard you work, your level of education, where you grew up, your profession, or even who you know. Instead, your abundance or lack of money is determined primarily by your subconscious mind!

This may seem counter-intuitive, but the more you think about it, the more it makes sense. Have you ever heard stories of people who won the lottery and had millions of dollars, only to lose everything and be broke again, sometimes in less than a year? There are many such stories out there, and they all reflect the importance of subconscious belief systems; for example, I have heard that something like 80% of lottery winners lose their money within 5 years. In fact, there was a story in the news in early 2007 about the man who won a $330,000,000+ Powerball Jackpot, the largest ever in history, and yet a few years later he had lost it all!

On the other hand, Donald Trump accumulated a real estate empire and had a net worth that was in the hundreds of millions, if not billions of dollars, when his company went bankrupt. He went from having billions of dollars, to bankruptcy...but within a few years, he had accumulated even more wealth than he had before! What's going on here?

To borrow and extend a metaphor from T Harv Eker, these things happen because the level of wealth and prosperity that we enjoy is determined primarily by our **subconscious financial thermostat**. The subconscious financial thermostat is an insightful and appropriate metaphor, because the way the Universe works with our level of wealth and prosperity is exactly the same way that the air conditioning and heating systems work in our home.

In my home, I have a thermostat that I set for the desired level of temperature; for example, 72°F. Does this mean that the temperature inside can never get higher than 72° or lower than 72°? Of course not; there are a variety of reasons why the temperature may rise or fall below this setting. For example, if it is an extremely hot day and I have a whole bunch of people come over to my home, it will likely get very hot inside, and the temperature will rise above 72°. But, when the temperature goes above 72°, the climate control system in my home will recognize this and turn on the air conditioning. The air-conditioning will stay on and cool the home until the temperature falls back down to 72°.

Similarly, if it is a very cold day and I leave the windows open, then the temperature inside will fall below 72°. But, the climate control system will recognize this, and it will turn on the heat until the temperature rises back to 72°.

If something extreme happens with the weather, the temperature may temporarily rise significantly above or below 72°, and it may take a long time for the control system to bring it back to the 72° setting on the thermostat. For example, if it is 0°F outside and snowing, and I leave all my windows and doors open and go on a trip for a week, then it is likely that it will get very cold inside, even if the heat has been running nonstop. When I return home from my trip, I may find that it is 40° inside, even though the heat has been running for a week. But, after I close the doors and windows, the temperature will begin to rise quickly and soon it will be 72° again. No matter what, even if there are extreme temporary fluctuations in the temperature, sooner or later the temperature will be exactly what the setting on the thermostat indicates.

The level of wealth and prosperity that we enjoy in our lives works exactly in the same way. The sum total of all your subconscious programs about wealth, money, and abundance serve to create a subconscious financial thermostat whose setting indicates the average level of wealth that you will experience in your life.

Of course it is not only possible but inevitable that the level of wealth you experience will sometimes vary from this setting. But, over time, the Universe is like the climate control system in your home. If the level of wealth you are experiencing varies from what you are subconsciously programmed for, the Universe will accommodate you and give you new experiences such that, over time, you end up with (on average) the level of wealth and prosperity that you are programmed for.

Thus, if you end up having more wealth than you are programmed for – for example, if you are programmed for poverty and win the lottery – then the Universe will find ways to take this money from you, and you will lose it. On the other hand, if you end up with less wealth than you are programmed to have – as in the example of Donald Trump – then the Universe has no choice but to find ways to send you more money. This is as reliable and consistent as gravity.

So can we use a technique such as Theta Healing to reprogram ourselves for a higher level of prosperity and wealth? Of course we can! We just need to identify and fix the bugs in our subconscious programming that are holding down the setting on our subconscious financial thermostat.

Resetting the Subconscious Financial Thermostat

So how do you program yourself for a higher level of wealth and prosperity? How exactly does one change the setting on the subconscious financial thermostat?

Quite simply, every time you fix "bugs" in your subconscious software that give you a reason to be poor or avoid wealth, your thermostat rises. In the example below, the client and practitioner work together to reprogram the client's subconscious to reset his subconscious financial thermostat. The numbers used in the example are made up, and are presented only to clarify the result of the work being done.

Practitioner: *"What can I help you with?"*

Client: *"It seems like no matter how hard I work, I just cannot get ahead. I have a nice car and a bit of money in the bank, but every time I seem to be saving enough money to get ahead and make a serious investment, something comes up, and I find myself struggling to pay the bills again."*

At this point, the client's subconscious financial thermostat might have a setting of $10,000. In other words, he is programmed to have a net worth of approximately $10,000. If he has more money, the Universe – like a climate control system – will restrict his prosperity until it returns down to around $10,000. On the other side, if he has less, the Universe will turn up his prosperity until his net worth approaches $10,000.

Practitioner: *"OK, let us muscle test* 'It is safe for me to have enough money to get ahead'.*"*

The result is FALSE.

Practitioner: *"Why is it not safe for you to have enough money to get ahead?"*

Client: *"Well, my religion is important to me, I was always taught that you have to be poor to be close to God."*

Practitioner: *"OK, let us muscle test that –* 'I have to be poor to be close to God'.*"*

The result is TRUE. This explains one reason the client does not believe it is safe to have enough money to get ahead, as subconscious programs are telling him that he cannot be close to God unless he is poor.

Practitioner: *"Next, let us test* 'I know how to be rich and close to God at the same time'.*"*

The result is FALSE.

Practitioner: *"Would you like to learn?"*

Client: *"Yes, absolutely!"*

The practitioner then uses the Theta Healing technique to connect to the cosmic Internet and download new software into the client's subconscious mind, showing him how to be rich and close to God at the same time.

Practitioner: *"OK, retest* 'I know how to be rich and close to God at the same time'.*"*

The result is now TRUE.

Practitioner: *"Great! Now retest I have to be poor to be close to God."*

The result is now FALSE.

Practitioner: *"Wonderful! Now let us recheck our original problem program,* 'It is safe for me to have enough money to get ahead'.*"*

The result is now TRUE.

Client: *"Cool! Bring on the money!"*

The client's subconscious financial thermostat has now been reset by eliminating the program that says he has to be poor to be close to God. Now, instead of being set for $10,000, it might be set for $15,000, or even, $50,000, and he will have a much easier time accumulating enough savings to make some serious investments.

Learning to be a Powerful Manifester

"Thank you for the Theta Healing session yesterday. Pretty miraculous, to say the least! Why? In less than 24 hours I have experienced the following as a result of our session on releasing the blocks I had about money:

1. *Received $23,100 wire from a buyer of a car I sold*

2. *Received confirmation that the above buyer of car is also interested in my other car for $13,500 and wants to purchase it.*

3. *Received confirmation from a wholesale buyer in Colombia for a wrinkle cream I sell and had sent him a sample that he liked the product and is ready to make a large purchase of it.*

4. *Got a call from a former colleague that he saw on a computer he had lent me (and had taken back the day before), a wrinkle cream I sell (same one as above). He said he has overseas contacts of large email lists and wants to know if we can partner up to sell the cream overseas.*

5. *Received final confirmation on a business partner's affirmative answer to move forward with building my existing debt reduction business using a model he has used successfully in the past.*

The potential here is astronomical. And the good thing is also we will be helping people immensely while making a lot of money as well. Thanks again!"

HENRY J.
Miami Beach, Florida

- -

The topic of manifesting is rich and complex, and I could fill another book with manifesting tips, techniques, and processes. In a nutshell, manifesting is the process of attracting things outside of yourself into your life, such as more money, a new job, a romantic interest, a house, or anything else you might desire. For our purposes here I want to highlight the single most important and powerful component of our manifesting: *feeling!*

The Law of Attraction has gotten a lot of press and exposure, and many people are now aware that our own thoughts and focus have a powerful impact on the life experiences we manifest. However, empty thoughts – meaning those that are not backed up by a feeling – actually have very little power in the Universe. This is why it is possible for some people to say their mantras and affirmations a million times without any measurable changes in their lives. (There is an excellent description and explanation of this process in the book *The Divine Matrix* by Gregg Braden.)

To introduce a useful metaphor, imagine that your life is like a car. Your body and the world around you are the car itself, your thoughts are the steering wheel, and your feeling is the fuel in the gas tank. So in order for the car to go anywhere, you must have your thoughts steering you to where you want to go, and you must have sufficient feeling to fuel the journey towards your goal. If you have your thoughts properly lined up but without feeling, that's like a car that is pointed in the right direction but has no fuel...you will go nowhere and stay stuck in the same place! On the other hand, a car full of fuel without proper direction ends up driving in circles or going to the wrong place, which is what happens when you have lots of feeling empowering the wrong thoughts or inconsistent or contradictory thoughts.

In the previous chapter on using Theta Healing to reprogram the subconscious to heal emotional issues, it was mentioned that one of the reasons that subconscious reprogramming is so powerful is because it literally changes how you feel about things. So, by being able to change the subconscious programs that create your feelings, you can literally create and install new feelings with Theta Healing, turbo-charging your ability to manifest the things you really want in your life. And when your subconscious mind and your conscious mind are on the same page and your thoughts and your feelings are working together, miracles happen!

Common Blocks to Wealth and Prosperity

Because prosperity is such a common topic for Theta Healing work, I have worked with many different people on all sorts of prosperity issues. I categorize most of the bugs blocking us from prosperity into four major areas:

- Becoming a Rich Person.
- Reasons to Be Poor.
- Struggle and Sacrifice.
- The True Nature of Money.

When I work with people on prosperity issues, I usually check them on some basic programs in all four of these areas before we get into the nitty-gritty of their issues, because so many of us have common programs blocking us from wealth and abundance.

Sadly, lack of prosperity is also the most common excuse I get from people for not trying or continuing with Theta Healing. This can be frustrating because I know that with the right subconscious reprogramming, **everyone** can turn up their subconscious financial thermostats and enjoy more wealth and prosperity.

Taking the Next Step: Increasing YOUR Prosperity

Tweaking the subconscious to increase prosperity may seem overly simple and too good to be true, but this is really how the Universe works...the fastest path to prosperity is to increase the setting of your subconscious financial thermostat!

Usually the fastest way to increase the setting on your subconscious financial thermostat is to do private sessions to clear your blocks to prosperity and success. If you cannot afford private sessions, you would be well served to attend group events such as *The Wealth Club*, which are inexpensive group healing tele-seminars I run as part of my *Formula for Miracles*™ VIP Club to help you clear your blocks to prosperity...and in a short time you should be able to manifest enough extra money to start doing private sessions! (See Appendix B for more information on the VIP Club.)

Additionally, I have developed special audio programs that combine binaural beats technology with specially charged Theta Healing energy to actually clear your subconscious blocks just by listening to them – it's Theta Healing in a bottle! The first such program developed is *Unleash Your Inner Millionaire*, which includes not only presentations of the most powerful hidden secrets to manifesting and the Law of Attraction, but also several hours worth of Theta Healing to clear your blocks to prosperity as you listen! (You can find more information on this technology and the Formula for Miracles™ audio programs in Appendix A.)

You will also get an enormous amount of benefit from learning to do the Theta Healing process so you can use it on yourself and the people close to you. (Please see Appendix C for more information on the Basics of Theta Healing seminar.)

For more information, please visit the Web site *www.Theta HealingLA.com*.

Chapter 12: Theta Healing for Relationships

"I wanted to thank you for your healing session, and share with you that a true miracle has occurred -- much to my shock and delight. Within 5 days of our session to lift roadblocks in my romantic life, I was approached by a stunning young woman with whom I share many spiritual and personal interests, and we have begun dating! I was honestly skeptical that anything remarkable would happen in the aftermath of our Theta Healing session, expecting that my love life would continue to be more of the same, a long and painful struggle to find someone special in the vast crowd. And then my jaw dropped when I unexpectedly received an email from a beautiful girl who had found some old, forgotten profile I had put up on an Internet dating site months ago. She reached out to me and within two days we had met and have begun a wonderful new relationship. It is of course too early to say where things are headed for the long term, but we are both enjoying each other's company and the new adventure we have begun. This is literally a quantum leap from the unfulfilling relationship cycle that I found myself trapped in over the past few years. So thank you, and may you receive everything that you have been seeking from the cosmos as well!"

Kamran P.

New York, New York

After health and prosperity, the next most common use of Theta Healing is for relationships. Like your health and your financial prosperity, the kinds of relationships you experience are attracted by your subconscious programs. If you are lacking love or respect, or wish to change any aspect of your relationships, you need to debug your subconscious relationship software!

We are involved in all sorts of relationships in our lives, many of which are not with other humans, such as our relationships with our cars and homes. Beyond the obvious love and romance relationships, some of the most important relationships in your life include:

- Your relationship with yourself.
- Your relationship with your home.
- Your relationship with the Universe/God.
- Your relationship with your car and other material possessions.
- Your relationships with your coworkers/bosses/business partners/clients.
- Your relationship with food, drugs, alcohol, etc.
- Your relationships with your animals.

There are three main application areas for working with relationships:

- Clearing the negative effects of relationships from the past (trauma, abuse, etc.)
- Improving existing relationships.
- Preparing for and then manifesting future relationships.

But no matter what the relationship, and no matter whether it is in the past, present, or the future, you can use the same techniques we use for health and prosperity to identify and fix the "bugs" in your subconscious software to improve your relationships.

Although the techniques described here can be applied to any kind of relationship – whether it is with another person, an entity such as a government or business, a place, an animal, or a higher spiritual power – for simplification of grammar we will assume that the relationship we are working with is between two people.

If You Love Something, Set It Free

When working on any sort of relationship with Theta Healing, my guiding principle is "If you love something, set it free." In other words, we want to release any and all of our pathological attachments and neediness that tell us that we have to get something from the other person.

Unfortunately, it is human nature to base our relationships – and especially our romantic relationships – on mutual dependence and neediness. Thus, relationships work only as long as we are getting what we think we need from another person, whether it is love, or attention, or validation, or simply a companion to stave off loneliness. However, as soon as we are threatened with not getting what we think we need from the other person, all the negativity, hostility, and resentment surfaces and things turn ugly fast. Our goal with Theta Healing is to transcend codependence and release all attachment to having other people be or not be a certain way or to give us something we think we need. Buddha says, "Attachment to result is the root of all suffering", and in terms of relationships, I would say that attachment to getting a particular result from a relationship is the cause of all break-ups!

A much healthier basis for a relationship is for two people to come together out of free will choice, each participating in the relationship because it fulfills and serves them, and not because they need something from the other person. There is a subtle but important distinction between being in a fear-based relationship – where you are afraid you will lose something you need or that something bad will happen if the relationship breaks up – and a love-based relationship, where the two people are involved because of mutual fulfillment and joy. In order to achieve this better kind of relationship, we must achieve a state of release, where each individual feels complete and whole separately, and does not need anything from the other person.

Note that **releasing someone is not necessarily the same as kicking them out of your life!** Even for the people you are closest to – friends, family, coworkers, etc. – you will be well served to release them and set them free, to allow your relationship to move to a higher level, free of neediness, dependence, attachment, and other negativity that is ultimately destructive to the relationship.

The following steps will lead you to achieve this state of release, allowing you to enjoy happy, mutually fulfilling relationships free of neediness, attachment, and codependence:

- Retrieving soul fragments and energy
- Releasing psychic/energetic cords, hooks, and other attachments
- Releasing hatred, resentments, and grudges

Retrieving Our Soul Fragments and Energy

What are soul fragments? Let's pause for a moment and discuss the nature of the soul and body. Our soul is an energy field that is actually much larger than the body itself; it is roughly spherical in shape and projects out a few feet in each direction from the body. Other commonly used terms for this soul energy include the morphogenic field, chi energy, and ki energy.

The physical size of somebody's soul energy field has no correlation to any other energetic properties, such as the power or size of the soul. Instead, it is more likely a measure of how much personal space is considered normal in the culture they grew up in.

Whenever we have a powerful emotional interaction with another person, we tend to exchange little bits of ourselves. In other words, we shave off a few tiny little soul fragments, and give the other person this energy, sometimes in exchange for a little bit of theirs. When we find ourselves thinking about someone frequently, especially if it seems to be more than is rational or reasonable, it is likely that we are carrying their soul fragments, or energy, within us.

You can call back the soul fragments and energy that you have given to another person, and likewise send their soul fragments back to them. Usually this is a simple and easy process with Theta Healing.

Cords, Hooks, and Other Energetic Attachments

We can develop what are known as energetic cords or psychic hooks to another person. This means that our energy is attached to their energy, and these attachments are pathological and usually just drain energy. People who are corded to us act like psychic vampires, sucking out our life force and weakening us.

It is quite common for us to have these sorts of cords, hooks, or other attachments to the important people in our lives, including our parents, our lovers, our children, and the people we work with. They are also commonly created during moments of great sympathy, such as when "our heart goes out" to someone.

If you want to find out if you have energetic attachments to another person, you can muscle test *"I have cords, hooks, or other attachments to <name>."* You should then follow this up by muscle testing *"<Name> has cords, hooks, or other attachments to me"*, since they can run in both directions.

As with all things in the subconscious mind, we want to be careful that there are no reasons these attachments are needed before they are removed. I have found that people commonly believe that if they release the attachments to someone they will lose them forever. So, if you are working on your relationship with Bob, muscle test the program *"If I release my attachments to Bob, I will lose him forever."* If it is TRUE, you need to install some new software into the subconscious so these attachments can be quickly and easily released. (Any psychic worth their salt can pull psychic cords and hooks, but it requires subconscious reprogramming to ensure that they stay gone and are not recreated.)

A good metaphor for these energetic cords, hooks, and other attachments is to imagine two people playing as a team in a two-on-two basketball game. For our example, let us assume these two people are Bob and Mary. For whatever reason, they start the basketball game with blindfolds on. Because they are blindfolded, they will probably find it useful to hold a rope between them, so they can use the rope and pull on it to determine where their teammate is at any time. So, in this circumstance, having a rope that attaches Bob and Mary might actually be useful to them as long as they are blindfolded, even though this rope will slow them down and might cause them to trip or fall.

But, once they are able to remove the blindfolds, then of course Bob and Mary do not want to continue to be roped together. Energetic cords, hooks, and other attachments work in the same way. We may have subconscious programs that tell us they are necessary, but if we can find better ways to achieve the same result, we can release them quickly and permanently. They are just more bugs in the software!

It is incredible to see the change in people after releasing their energetic attachments to important people in their lives. Often people who "push our buttons" do so because we are attached to their energy, so even the littlest things can set off episodes of intense emotion. Sometimes just de-cording people with Theta can completely transform a relationship, perhaps even saving a marriage or a business partnership that has been on the rocks.

Resentment, Hatred, and Grudges

"I had minimal success with Theta...until I started working with Brent, his system and methodology was impeccable, I had major disruptions in my life, child hood orphanage, sexual abuse at a young age, physical abuse and never did well in school... I was NOT speaking to my mom nor sister for at least 6 months, major discord and anger and dysfunction in my family.

*I started working with Brent, since then shifts have happened, major shifts, since Brent, I have been home to see mom (she has not stopped calling or emailing me since) she cooked me dinner, and expressed being my friend, and I have been able to let go of anger and hurt and blame, **no one** has been able to help me this way. I have done energy healings that have left me sitting in my stuff, pain, anger, disappointment, wasted money, but* *working with Brent I have seen immediate results and have been happier in my over all life.*

I still have a ways to go but I am doing better than I have in 35 years, I still have issues, but the nice thing is I don't stay there, whatever Brent did, mind you I was emotionally burning. I am able to shift and move beyond. I don't stay angry or moody...It's incredible because opportunities for further healing and evaluation of my life have become more available to me, since working with Brent. When I tell you that Malice, resentment, emotional pain and discord ruled my life, it did. Since working with Brent this has all shifted."

KIMBERLY B.
Germantown, Maryland

Many of us hold a tremendous number of subconscious resentments, hatred, and grudges towards other people, events, and entities (governments, businesses, etc.) While many of these may seem justified in our minds, whatever the justification, resentments, hatreds, and grudges are not good for us. At the least they will make us feel bad, and can even cause serious health problems.

Although we may at first be reluctant to remove our negative feelings about those that really seem to deserve it, we need to understand that no matter how well justified we may think these feeling are, these negative feelings are damaging to us. If you are extremely angry with an action that the government has taken, you may feel justified in holding subconscious programming that says you hate and resent the government. Unfortunately, holding these negative programs in your subconscious software does not help; in fact, they can hurt you, and can even make you sick.

For whatever reason you think you need to hold these resentments, hatred, and grudges, there is always a better way to achieve the same result without the bad feelings. If you wish to oppose the government, you may do so, but it is not necessary to hold damaging negative programs in your subconscious to do this effectively. However, your subconscious software may believe it is necessary. For example, if you muscle test TRUE to the program *"I need to hate the government to get it to change"*, then you should probably download the alternate program *"I know how to get the government to change without hate."* The same result of effectively opposing the government is achieved, but without the negative programming in your subconscious and its resulting damage to your mind and body.

Many times people will hold resentment and old abuse and hatred in the abdominal region. I have actually seen one of my students drop nearly an inch on his waist size with 30 minutes of healing simply by clearing resentments out of his subconscious software! And one of Vianna's students reported that she dropped a full two inches off her waist overnight after spending two hours clearing resentments with Theta Healing.

For any important person in your life – we will continue to use Bob as an example – it is probably a good idea to debug your subconscious software until you muscle test FALSE to *"I resent Bob"*, *"I hate Bob"*, and *"I hold a grudge against Bob."*

Sometimes you can see dramatic transformations in a personal relationship after releasing resentment, hatred, and grudges. One day I did about five minutes of Theta Healing with my friend Ben while we were sitting in a car waiting for someone. We only had a few minutes, so all we did was clear his subconscious resentment, hatred, and grudges he was holding towards his parents. Yet the next time I saw him, he remarked on how incredible it was that his relationship with his parents had changed and become noticeably smoother and more mature for no apparent reason. (Of course, the reason was readily apparent to me!)

We Powerfully Influence Other People with Subconscious Signals

It is interesting to note that most of us are completely unaware of the powerful influence that our own subconscious programs have on other peoples' behavior. Have you ever known someone who seemed to act differently – possibly including multiple different dispositions as well as vocabularies and manners – depending on the people they are around?

Of course, we all do this to some degree, but this behavior is much more pronounced in some than in others. And many of us have found ourselves acting subtly different when we are around certain people. It is generally not a conscious choice; instead, it just seems natural to be in a different mood, to use different word choices, to take different perspectives, or to talk about different topics depending on who we are with.

It may not be immediately obvious on a conscious level, but human bodies act like little broadcasting stations that are continuously transmitting our subconscious programs about other people to their subconscious receivers. And it does not seem to matter whether we are physically with a person, talking on the phone, or even chatting over a computer network. The effect is the same: it seems natural for us to change our behavior around different people because we are continuously being bombarded by signals sent from their subconscious to ours!

Of course, we all have free will, and we may choose to ignore or act upon these signals. Nonetheless, these signals often have a powerful impact on our behavior.

There are no hard and fast rules for the exact extent of how much a signal will affect another person. But sometimes changing your own subconscious programs about other people can have an immediate and dramatic influence upon their behavior.

About Soul-mates

A lot of people are fixated on the concept of a "soul-mate". Is there such a thing? Yes, but soul-mates are probably not exactly what you think they are.

We have many different soul-mates, because all the term "soul-mate" means is that we have a lot of common experience with another person. Usually most of these experiences are from other times and places. If you have ever met someone and feel as if you have known them all your life, you are probably right...just not your *current* life!

It is quite common for our soul-mates to show up for important events in our lives, even if we do not recognize them. For example, if you are injured in a serious car accident, the person that hit you is likely one of your soul-mates, although you probably do not recognize him from this lifetime.

Why do we run into our soul-mates like this? When it comes to socializing, we tend to act on the subconscious level just like we act on the conscious level. For example, if you are going to go to the movies, you will probably not go to the grocery store and grab a random person and ask them to go with you; this seems strange. Instead, you will probably call one of your friends.

Similarly, on the level of the subconscious mind, when you are creating some important experience in your life, you will tend to connect with and use other soul energies that are familiar to you: your soul-mates!

We have many different soul-mates, but not all of them are unavailable or even compatible, and some are not even human. (There are funny Theta Healing stories of people who have manifested soul-mates but did not specify the species, and ended up with a really nice dog or cat showing up at their doorstep.) So, just because somebody is one of your soul-mates does not mean that they are a good match for you. However, because they are your soul-mate, you will likely feel very comfortable around them, and this is probably one reason why you ended up being with them. But just because someone is your soul-mate does not mean that you will like them, or that they are compatible with you, or even good for you. In fact, incompatible soul-mates can make you absolutely miserable.

You also need to be careful when calling in an important soul-mate, such as a life partner. This is because when you do a Theta Healing manifestation to call a soul-mate into your life, you always get somebody that is matched properly to the vibration and programs you are carrying in your subconscious software at the point you do the manifestation. So, if you know that you still have a lot of work to do on yourself to release old wounds and anger about past relationships, you may want to wait before you manifest your life partner, because if you do it now you will probably get someone who has similar negative programs in their subconscious.

Once you feel you are in a really good place in your life, and think it would be wonderful to have someone of a similar vibration to spend your time with, it is a good time to manifest your soul-mate partner.

Taking the Next Step: Improving Your Relationships

Whether your goal is to clear trauma from past relationships, or to attract your soul-mate, or new business partners, or any other sort of relationship, Theta Healing is a powerful resource to get your subconscious mind working for you instead of against you. As with health and prosperity, Theta Healing private sessions and learning to do Theta Healing by taking the Basics of Theta Healing Seminar will give you the tools to transform all of your relationships for the rest of your life.

Additionally, I regularly run a group healing tele-seminar called *The Love Club* where we do healing on common subconscious blocks to fulfilling and loving relationships. You can register for *The Love Club* online at *www.ThetaHealingLA.com*, or get live access to all the *Love Club* events and download recent recordings as part of the *Formula for Miracles VIP Club* (please see Appendix B for more information.)

Further, you can take advantage of the *Formula for Miracles*™ technology through the audio program *In Love for a Lifetime*, which automatically clears hundreds of the most common blocks to love, romance, sex, and intimacy. (To get more information on *In Love for a Lifetime* and the *Formula for Miracles*™ technology, please see Appendix A.)

Chapter 13: Theta Healing for Spirituality, Healing, and Intuitive Ability

"My name is Victoria and I have been seeking answers to my spirituality and emotional self for more than twenty years now. I have traveled to other parts of the world learning other languages and cultures and have immersed myself in many books on the subject. I have also studied all kinds of modalities such as astrology, numerology, tarot, aura and chakra readings, channeling, meditation, etc.

In twenty years, I have not experienced anything that works faster and more complete than Theta Healing. It takes the guesswork out of healing! It catapults you ahead to where you feel you are finally "caught up" to where you want to be. You no longer need to struggle. The steps to enlightenment become joyful instead of tedious.

There isn't any area that Theta did not help me. Relationships are smoother, work and finances are more fun, my outlook on life is shinier. I no longer feel handicapped by my own self-doubt and fears. I have always been an optimistic person and have relied a lot on faith to pull me through."

VICTORIA C.
Reno, Nevada

The fourth major area that people commonly address with Theta Healing and other methods of subconscious reprogramming is spirituality, healing, and ascension. If we truly wish to be closer to God (or Goddess or Source or the

Universe or whatever concept you prefer), we simply need to reprogram our subconscious software to fix the bugs that keep us mired in the low-vibration duality of our human existence. For example, if you have the subconscious program *"I have to meditate for 40 years before God will hear my prayers"*, you will want to fix that so that God can start hearing your prayers now.

One of my favorite things about the Theta Healing technique is that you can use it to make yourself better at Theta Healing or any other modality – and it really works! If you have bugs in your subconscious software telling you that you cannot heal or that healing is dangerous or that people will think you are crazy if you develop psychic ability, these bugs will block you from being a proficient healer, even if you do not believe them in your conscious mind.

Not only that, you can even use Theta Healing to manifest a successful Theta Healing practice, something that Terry and I and many others have done. It works so well, it feels like cheating!

I believe that anyone who is going to learn to do Theta Healing (or any other similar modality) should prepare for the training seminars by clearing subconscious blocks to becoming a highly proficient healing practitioner. If you are running programs in your subconscious mind that tell you that it is not possible to heal instantly, or that you will be killed for being a healer, or anything like that, you will likely have a difficult time learning to heal. I typically see over 90% of my students graduate from the Basic Theta Healing class. The others do not finish the class not because they lack the proper inherent talent, but simply because they still have too many bugs in their subconscious software about becoming a healer.

Some common programs that people carry that interfere with their ability to evolve spiritually and learn to perform healing and miracles of their own include the following:

- I will be punished/killed/excommunicated if I heal people.
- I must give up one of my physical senses to develop psychic sense. (This program is the basis of the archetype of the blind prophet.)
- I must use my own energy to heal others. (This is dangerous and unnecessary!)
- I must take on somebody else's illness or injury before I can heal it.
- I must experience an injury or illness before I can heal it.
- It is wrong for me to accept money for doing healing work.
- Those that do healing always eat first. (This is one of the reasons that people sometimes gain weight when they start doing healing work.)
- I cannot be close to God/evolve spiritually and be with a human partner at the same time.

It is extremely common for people to carry traumas on the history level and the genetic level from having had horrible things happen from doing healing in the past. It is important to identify, resolve and release these traumas and wounds and the negative subconscious programs associated with them before training to become a healing practitioner.

Further, I am continually amazed at how powerful and effective subconscious reprogramming is in helping people to develop their intuitive senses. Often times, the only reason my students have difficulty developing their intuitive abilities is because they simply lack the proper subconscious software, and this can be installed in seconds.

For example, if you muscle test FALSE to the program "*I know how to see intuitively in my mind's eye*", then you will probably have a very difficult time developing your clairvoyant (psychic seeing) sense. Fortunately, it is a simple matter of downloading and installing the proper subconscious software so that you can then muscle test TRUE to this program. Many times in my Theta Healing seminars and practice groups I have seen people struggling with their intuitive abilities, yet after a few simple changes in their subconscious software, it turns on immediately and suddenly they can do clear and accurate psychic readings!

Using the Proper Energy for Healing

Another important aspect of preparing the subconscious for doing healing work is to ensure that you have the proper internal software installed to connect to the right energies for doing healing. There are many kinds of energies in the Universe and they all can be used for healing, but some are much more effective and easier to use than others, and some carry serious consequences and risks if used improperly.

Given that Theta Healing is really just a form of prayer – albeit a highly technical and sophisticated form of prayer – it may seem funny that there is a "right" and a "wrong" way to pray. But I see effective healing as a consciousness or prayer technology, where if you do it correctly you can get consistent, amazing results without any side effects. On the other hand, if you pray improperly, it will do nothing, and can even cause problems.

The simplest and easiest way to heal others, which nearly all people can do without any training, is to give up your own energy to another person. This is an almost instinctive thing for mothers to do when their children are sick. Mothers will tend to bend over their children and hold them or caress them and actively will that they send their own energy and life force into their child's. This can work, and sometimes you can get good results, but it is not the ideal way to heal, because doing so depletes the person giving the energy.

Instead, with a little bit of training and installation of the proper subconscious software, it is possible to connect to the unlimited energy supply of the Universe itself. When we connect to this proper energy, our healing not only occurs without depleting us, but it tends to be more powerful, more immediate and to stay longer. So, while it is a noble concept to give of your own energy to help another, it is truly not necessary, and in fact is a bad idea.

For example, imagine that you are driving when you see one of your friends pulled over along the side of the road, his car stalled. You ask him what happened and he tells you that he ran out of gas. Now, if the only way you know to get gas into his car is to siphon some out of your own tank, this will work, but you will have less gas for yourself. And, if you give him too much gas out of your car, your car will stall instead!

If gas were healing, we would all be equipped with an infinite gas can in the trunk of our cars. If you know about this infinite gas can and know how to access it, you do not ever have to give anyone any gas out of your tank, because you can simply show them how to access the infinite gas can they have in their own trunk. This is a much better solution!

So what is the right energy to connect to for healing, and how do you know that you have successfully connected to it? Let us diverge for a minute into a little bit of metaphysical terminology.

Nothing here is meant to be dogma or interpreted as the absolute right way to do things. The model presented below is simply one theory and a set of accompanying terminology to describe the various energies in the Universe that can be used for healings and manifestations. While this model and terminology have proved extremely useful and seem to really work and be "true", it is important to avoid getting into arguments over semantics or quibbling over the details of the exact nature of metaphysics and effective prayer. There are certainly other people with deep understandings of metaphysics who use completely different models and terminology, so nothing presented below should be inferred to mean that other explanations, understandings or terminology are wrong or irrelevant. They are simply different.

As an engineer and a practical person, I use Theta Healing because **it just works!** I do not believe in Theta Healing and the power of subconscious reprogramming out of some romantic, idealistic notion of being a healer or lightworker. Instead, I believe in Theta Healing and the Seven Planes of Existence model (described below) for the same reason I believe in my car: I find my car to be a useful device, since when I drive my car, it takes me places I want to go. Hence, you could say I *believe* in my car because it takes me to the places I want to go. But if my car did not work or did not take me to the places I want to go, I would get rid of it. Similarly, I believe in Theta Healing and the Seven Planes of Existence because they work and take me places I want to go – and if they stopped working, I would get rid of them too!

I cannot currently offer any "good science" proof to support the metaphysical theories presented here. However, I can offer significant anecdotal evidence and personal experience that indicates that these theories are based in truth, because they really work in practice.

The Seven Planes of Existence

Vianna Stibal has developed a powerful metaphysical model called the **Seven Planes of Existence**. Everything in the entire Universe is made up of these seven planes, all working together.

There are certainly other valid terminologies and models which may use different meanings for the words or different numbers of planes. Instead of seven, it would be equally valid to divide up the planes into 12 or 24 or any other arbitrary number, simply by dividing or combining and redefining the exact meaning of what each plane is. The labels and numbers we use in this model do not change what is actually out there in the Universe, but they are convenient abstractions for us to use.

So what are the Seven Planes of Existence? A quick summary of each plane is presented below.

The First Plane of Existence: Rocks, Crystals, Minerals, and Mother Earth

The First Plane is the plane of the rocks, crystals and minerals. It is the plane of the non-organic molecules (that is, molecules lacking a carbon-based structure.)

There are many powerful healing modalities that use rocks and crystals and minerals. It is fascinating that the reason that crystal layouts are powerful tools for past life regressions and healing is that they can be used to put you into a deep theta state!

We must have the First Plane in our bodies in order to survive, because our bones are made out of minerals. Further, minerals are required for many different important bodily functions. Many people are chronically mineral deficient and because they do not have the proper First Plane energies (minerals) in their bodies, they often have health problems as a result.

Minerals are especially important to the process of Theta Healing because a person who is mineral deficient will find it difficult to muscle test clearly. I have often seen people who started a session unable to muscle test, but after drinking some water with ionized minerals, they started muscle testing clearly and easily. (Magnesium deficiency is particularly common.)

Further, because the process of performing energy healing depletes the minerals in the body, people who do a lot of energy healing work generally have higher than average requirements for mineral intake.

The Second Plane of Existence: Plants and Nature Spirits

The Second Plane is the plane of the nature spirits and plants, manifested physically as organic molecules (that is, molecules based on a carbon structure.) Healing modalities that use herbs, plants, vitamins, and yeast are all strongly connected to the Second Plane.

We must have the Second Plane in our bodies in order to survive, because most of our body tissues are composed of organic molecules. Of course, we must eat plants and vitamins in order to continually provide a new supply of organic molecules for our body to provide energy and to rebuild the body's tissues.

I have often wondered how it was that primitive man managed to survive living in a difficult, dangerous world without any of the advantages of technology or modern civilization. Vianna teaches that primitive humans were so in touch with nature that they could telepathically communicate with plants. For example, if a primitive human was sick, the plants themselves would tell the person what they should eat as a natural remedy. In our modern world, our bodies and minds are too polluted to access this ability, but the talent to communicate with plants is still latent within us.

Examples of healing modalities that are strongly connected to the Second Plane are homeopathy and any system that uses plants or herbs as remedies.

The Third Plane of Existence: The Animal World

The Third Plane is the plane of the animal world. Thus, we as humans are most strongly connected to the Third Plane. It is the plane of motion and movement, as manifested through the physical structures of the muscles and their constituent proteins which move our bodies through space.

Much like the First Plane and the Second Plane, we must have the Third Plane in our bodies in order to survive. Just as we need minerals and vitamins, we also need a constant supply of many different amino acids to create the various proteins made inside the body. In nutrition, what are known as the essential amino acids are a set of amino acids that must be in our diet because they cannot be synthesized in the human body. In fact, the first (physical) layer of our DNA is really just a big recipe book for how to create different proteins out of these amino acids.

An example of a healing modality that uses the Third Plane is traditional Western Medicine, with its drugs and surgeries. Western Medicine is a Third Plane healing system because it involves physically moving and changing the body with drugs and surgeries in order to heal illness and injury.

An example of an alternative Third Plane modality is amino acid therapy, where a nutritional specialist works with clients to find the proper amino acid supplements to improve their health. Massage, yoga, and physical therapy are other good examples of Third Plane healing modalities.

The Fourth Plane of Existence: The Spirit World

The Fourth Plane is the plane of spirits; it is where our ancestors reside, and where we go between lifetimes. Since we as humans are spirits incarnated into a physical body, we all have a strong connection to the Fourth Plane.

Many traditional healing modalities passed to us from more primitive times are strongly connected to the Fourth Plane, including but not limited too many Native American and Polynesian healing methods. A good example of a healing modality that is strongly connected to the Fourth Plane is shamanism.

One popular use of psychic readings is to contact our ancestors or others who have passed on ahead of us. By using a technique such as Theta Healing to reprogram our subconscious to thin the "veil" between our physical world and the spirit world of the Fourth Plane, we can learn to readily access those who have gone before us, so that death transforms from a permanent loss into a change of form. In fact, one of the exercises taught in the Advanced Theta Healing seminar is how to use Theta to contact your ancestors!

The Fifth Plane: The Realm of Duality (Good and Evil)

The Fifth Plane, also known as the Astral Plane, is quite an interesting place, as it is the plane of duality and polarity. It is the plane of good and evil, where the forces of light and the forces of darkness wage an eternal war. It is the plane of the gods and goddesses, the angels and the demons, the ascended masters and the Councils of Twelve.

Many of our traditional religions and spiritual teachings are strongly rooted in the Fifth Plane. It is a plane of duality, where there is a right way and a wrong way, a right path and a wrong path. If you are connected to Fifth Plane intelligence, it may tell you things such as you must live or be a certain way in order to be close to God. If you are told "You are the chosen one" or "you are the only hope", this message is probably not truly from Creator/God/Source/All That Is, but rather from Fifth Plane energy.

Before Vianna had an understanding of the Seven Planes of Existence and the various energies we can use for healing, Theta Healing was also a Fifth Plane-centric modality, and years ago most Theta Healing practitioners were using Fifth Plane energies (in particular angels) for their healings.

An example of a Fifth Plane modality is angel healing, where practitioners call in various types of angels to perform healings and manifestations for their clients. Angels are a lot of fun to play with, and one of the exercises taught in the Basic Theta

Healing seminar is how to use Theta Healing to contact your guardian angels.

The Sixth Plane: The Laws of the Universe

The Sixth Plane is the home of the Laws of the Universe, which regulate, balance and control how all things manifest and interact with each other. Examples of some of the Laws from the Sixth Plane are the Law of Attraction, the Law of Gravity, the Law of Time, the Law of Magnetics, and the Law of Cause and Effect. The Sixth Plane is also the home of numbers, mathematics, and the Akashic Records (or Hall of Records.)

When I was younger I used to think that I was a great software engineer because I was so smart and worked really hard. Now I understand that a large part of my talent was that I am a natural Sixth Plane intuitive. With software, I've always known intuitively how it works, how to create it, and how to fix it. I know that my father and both of my grandfathers had a similar talent, and so it was natural for us to become engineers.

I do not necessarily mean to classify myself in the same category as these great men, but all the renowned scientists of the world – Newton, Einstein, Tesla, etc. – were natural Sixth Plane intuitives.

Examples of modalities that are strongly connected to the Sixth Plane include astrology, numerology, sacred geometry, vibration machines, and sound and light therapies.

The Seventh Plane: All That Is

The Seventh Plane is the Everything: the All That Is, Ever Was, and Ever Will Be. It is all of the other planes combined, the

God/Goddess/Source essence, the Alpha and the Omega, the Up and Down, the Here and the There and the space in between. It is the energy of creation itself, the infinite intelligence of the Universe expressed through itself, as itself, by itself. Using the energy of the Seventh Plane, truly anything is possible, including instant healings of "incurable" diseases and instant manifestations of material objects.

If you doubt that using Seventh Plane energy can easily accomplish anything you can imagine, just remember that whatever it is you think is hard to do, it pales in comparison with the difficulty and sophistication required to create the Universe itself!

Do you really think it is that difficult to heal cancer, compared to creating the Universe?

Do you really think it is that difficult to manifest a million dollars, compared to creating the Universe?

Do you really think it is that difficult to find a compatible and loving life partner, compared to creating the Universe?

Of course not!

The best example of a modality strongly connected to the 7th Plane is Theta Healing.

(Those interested in learning more about the Seven Planes of Existence are strongly encouraged to take the Theta Healing seminars, where the Planes are examined and explained in much more detail.)

Working with Animals

"Max, my cat was not his usual extremely buttery sweet self, in fact his fur had lost all of it is healthy fluffiness and instead looked oily and

separated in a most unhealthy way. I finally called Brent in an extremely upset state when Max (who has been FIV positive for a few years) bit at me and a friend and proceeded to pant and hang his mouth open in an uncontrollable way, I thought he was dying. Immediately after the session with Brent, Max began to look better, his usual relaxed temperament returned and his fur returned once again to his fluffy self. I am blessed to be able to say 6 months have passed and Max is still beautiful and healthy thanks to Brent and Theta."

NIKI G.
Los Angeles, California

As an animal lover, one of my favorite things about Theta Healing is that it works so well on animals.

Just like humans, animals hold subconscious programs inside of them that create every aspect of their existence. So, just like a human, if an animal gets sick or has some other problem in their life, there are programs in the animal's subconscious mind that are creating the problem.

However, unlike humans, animals generally do not require a lot of sophisticated "digging" to narrow in on the core of their issues. When working with humans, I prefer to do 60 or even 75 minute sessions to give us enough time to dig deep into their issues to find and release all the bugs in the subconscious software that are creating their problems. By contrast, I generally only do 30 minute sessions with animals, because they tend to have far less emotional baggage and trauma to work through before they can heal.

Animals – especially our pets – are natural healers, but the way that they know how to heal us is to take our injury or illness into themselves. A good example is my cat, Angel. After the surgery that left my arm frozen at the elbow, I became extremely sick with nausea and headaches from both the pain in my arm and all the drugs I was taking. Part of my discomfort resulted from being badly constipated, which is a common side effect of the pain killers I needed to take after the surgery.

Angel sat right next to me during my recovery, and he did everything he could to help me. (It is interesting that, before the surgery, Angel always curled up and slept next to me on my right side. Immediately after the surgery, he knew something was wrong with my right arm and started sleeping every night curled up next to my left side.) I did not realize it at the time, but Angel was taking on my sickness to heal me. And a few days after the surgery, he was obviously very sick. He was rushed to the vet, and the vet said that he was extremely ill because of severe constipation.

Fortunately, the vet had a treatment that worked to clear up his problem and Angel was back to his cute, healthy self in no time. But the vet said he had nearly died in his attempt to help heal me; indeed, he loved me so much, he was willing to die to help take away some of my pain. (I like to think that my other cat, Callisto, did not get sick not because she did not love me, but only because she had firmer boundaries.)

Working with animals is very similar to working with people, except that animals are not able to muscle test themselves. This is not a problem, however, as either the Theta practitioner or the animal's guardian can perform a proxy muscle test. Personally, I prefer to have the animal's human guardian do the proxy muscle testing, as I find it not only gives more accurate results, but also makes the person an interactive part of their animal's healing session.

Animals' subconscious issues are usually quite simple and straightforward. Animals are typically concerned only with safety, food, and taking care of the humans they love. After clearing an animal's subconscious of all the negative programs underlying an illness or injury or behavioral problem, I always like to muscle test, *"I need to have this problem for <person's name>."* This helps to ensure that the animal is not creating the problem in an attempt to help a human in the same way that Angel nearly died to help take away my pain.

On the whole, I have generally found that I get more consistent and more powerful healings on animals than on humans, probably because they tend to have fewer subconscious bugs to fix. This is not because human problems are inherently harder to heal, because all things are equally easy to heal with Theta Healing. Instead, the differences we encounter with the efficacy of Theta Healing on different illnesses, injuries and other life problems are created by the amount of subconscious programming that required debugging and have nothing to do with certain problems being inherently harder or easier than others. (After all, all of our problems are really easy to solve compared with creating the Universe!)

Taking the Next Step: Improving Your Own Intuitive and Healing Powers

If you are engaged in any sort of intuitive or healing modality (including but not limited to Reikki, hypnosis, massage, acupuncture, or Western medicine), you will likely find that a little bit of Theta Healing will go a long way to empowering your work and allowing you to get better results more quickly and more easily. I have a standard protocol I've developed that I use with healers of all sorts to clear any obligations or other limitations to the Seven Planes, as well as clearing common healer beliefs such as "I have to experience an injury or illness before I can heal it" or "I have to use my own energy to heal people."

Most of my Theta Healing students who come to my Basics of Theta Healing seminars are already healers of one sort or another, and nearly all of them find that not only does the seminar give them an amazing new tool to use with their clients, but it also makes their existing modality more powerful! And – as many of my students have experienced – once you have seen how easy and how powerful Theta Healing is, don't be surprised if it soon becomes your primarily modality!

Chapter 14: The Song of Life

"*After I did private Theta Sessions with Brent and attended his Theta classes, I have experienced several manifestations!!! My health improved miraculously (I had clean Blood test results concerning Lupus, Rhuematiod Arthritus, & kidney stones, and manifested a very reliable car - all within a week!*

I also did Theta on a friend of mine and she had an abundance of sales increases! I had only taken the first Theta class & tried it on her a few days after attending class! I have manifested even some money for some sessions for theta! Also, one day in a theta session, we did some feeling lucky theta, I won $50.00 on a Hot Spot ticket that same day for a $1.00!

There have been so many miracles in my life since my Theta sessions, Including seeing miracles on a puppy with parvo in which by that even he perked that same evening & lived after veterinarians had lost hope for him. Theta has changed my life significantly to my highest good!"

Thank-you Brent!

DYANI D.
San Dimas, California

As "real" as solid objects seem, the underlying truth is that everything in the Universe is composed of nothing more than frequencies. Even we humans are simply big piles of incredibly complex frequencies. Everything about us – our DNA, our bodies, our thoughts, everything – is made up of frequencies. There really are no such things as *solid* objects!

Physicists recognize and understand the truth of this. Did you know that so-called "solid" matter is something like 99.999+% empty space? The reason that solid objects seem solid is because of the electro-magnetic force. So, when you slap your hand against a "solid" wooden table, your hand is not stopped because your hand is solid or because the table is solid. Instead, what is really happening is that the electro-magnetic forces of the molecules in your hand interact with the electro-magnetic forces of the molecules in the table and they push each other apart. Hence, the table *feels* solid. This is exactly the same phenomena that happens if you try to push the "north" or "positive" ends of two magnets close together; the closer the magnets get, the stronger the magnetic force pushes them apart.

In high school chemistry we are taught the "solar system" model of the atom, where we think of solid particles known as electrons orbiting solid particles known as protons, with neutrons in the nucleus of the atom, much as the planets of our solar system orbit the Sun. However, quantum physics has proven that this is an inaccurate model of the atom. A better model has the electrons as waves or frequencies, much like the sound waves produced by a guitar string.

Hence, different chemical elements are not so much like little mini-solar systems as much as they are like different chords played on a guitar. A guitar chord is composed of different musical notes – frequencies – played in combination, and atoms are composed of different sub-atomic particles (electrons, neutrons, and protons) which serve as the atom's constituent notes. A comprehensive listing of the various known atoms (for example, carbon, oxygen, helium, etc.) can be found on the Periodic Table of the Elements.

Atoms combine into larger chemical structures called molecules, such as DNA and amino acids. These ever-larger building blocks connect together to create our tissues, organ systems, and entire bodies. Just as musical notes are combine to create chords, and chords are combined to create melodies and eventually entire songs, we are beings composed of many mind-bogglingly complex frequencies (notes) that all come together to create something (the song) which is far greater than the sum of its parts (the frequencies of the song's constituent notes.)

Different musical notes can resonate with each other or sound discordant, depending on how their frequencies combine. In the same way, when certain people seem to resonate with each other, we say that they are "on the same wavelength." Conversely, when two people have frequencies that do not match, they are "out of synch." Is not it incredible how our language reflects how we intuitively understand the importance of frequency and resonance to the point that we use mathematical terms to describe personal relationships?

There is a branch of mathematics and engineering called signal processing. Signal processing uses advanced mathematical techniques to break down and analyze the different frequencies in a signal. "Signal" in the abstract can have a very broad definition; a signal can be a musical song, or a radio transmission, or a human being.

Our minds and physical bodies are essentially a 3-dimensional manifestation of our underlying subconscious software. We humans are a huge and sophisticated combination of frequencies, and the sum total of all these signals combines into what I call our **song of life**.

Another popular metaphor is that of the *ripples in a pond*. Waves in the water move through a pond at certain frequencies, and each new pebble that is thrown into the pond creates new little ripples that move through the pond, slightly altering the frequencies of its waves.

When we use a technique such as Theta Healing, reaching the conscious theta brainwave gives us direct access to change the frequencies inside of ourselves that create our song of life. In this book, we have called this the "subconscious software". By using the theta brainwave and connecting to the Creative Source of the Universe, we can directly shift and alter the codes in the subconscious software to create a slightly different combination of frequencies that is our song of life. In the same way that editing the sheet music changes a song, we can reprogram our subconscious software and our song of life will change.

Energy healing and manifestation techniques such as Theta Healing are ways of using the power of our minds to directly alter the frequencies of our beings to achieve some result in our lives. To extend the pond metaphor, say that we have a pond and it has some waves in it, but the waves are too small. If we could throw **exactly** the right size rock into the pond at **exactly** the right time with **exactly** the right force, we could make the waves in the pond bigger or smaller or faster or slower, as we chose.

Theta Healing can be understood as a quick and easy way to bring in exactly the right frequencies to make the changes you desire in your song of life. For example, if there are codes in your subconscious software that are creating a life with physical illness, you need to bring in the right frequencies of the right strength to change those codes and create a new life without the illness. This is possible because we all have this ability hidden inside of us. In other words, every single one of us has the ability to access infinite intelligence within us (the Seventh Plane energy) to make exactly the changes in our own codes that we desire. And this is why everybody, no matter what our age, talents, background, intelligence, career, or religious affiliation, can learn to access the Seventh Plane energy and create miraculous healings and manifestations.

For example, say that you muscle test TRUE to the program, *"I have to be poor to be close to God."* When you do this, the frequencies inside you are vibrating such that when you say these words, they resonate with the codes in the subconscious, creating stronger electromagnetic fields around your body in the same way that throwing another rock into the pond can make the waves bigger. Then, when a Theta Healing practitioner changes this subconscious belief, the right frequency is taken from the cosmic Internet and combined with your existing frequencies so that you now no longer resonate with the program *"I have to be poor to be close to God."* Explained in terms of the ripples in the pond analogy, it is like throwing a rock of just the right size into the pond at just the right time so that it cancels out and stops the waves in the pond.

The magic of language and the human brain are such that the meaning of our words is translated into a specific set of frequencies that accesses codes inside us. Thus, when we have the program, *"I have to be poor to be close to God"* in our subconscious software, these frequencies will create a song of life without wealth. If you do not like your song of life, rewrite the music (i.e. modify the constituent frequencies by reprogramming the subconscious software) and change the song!

When new frequencies are combined within our subconscious, they combine with the frequencies already inside of us to change our life experiences, much as adding, deleting, or changing the notes in a song changes the song.

Science Has Proven that Everything is Just Frequency

Whenever you ingest any kind of substance – a drug, a food, a nutritional supplement, anything – the substance has an effect on the body by interacting with special chemical receptors on our cells. When the substance interacts with the cell's receptors, it triggers specific responses in the body.

Let us take caffeine as an example. When you drink coffee, the caffeine is digested by the intestines and circulated through the body via the blood stream. When the caffeine chemicals are in the blood stream, they interact with certain cells that have special receptors for caffeine. When these receptors are activated, it causes the body to respond in the ways we are familiar with, including higher alertness, a feeling of being more awake, and perhaps shaking and nervousness if we overdo it.

If all this talk of frequencies seems strange, you may be shocked to hear that scientific experiments have proven that chemicals affect our bodies simply by emitting frequencies, **not** by direct physical contact between molecules!

We have a misconception of how chemicals work when they enter our bodies. We think that the bloodstream carries them through the body, that these chemicals (caffeine in our example) physically bounce around and "run into" cells that have special receptors for caffeine. This is **not** the case! Did you know that if we actually had to wait for chemicals in the bloodstream to physically make contact with the various cells in the body to trigger them, it would take on average 48 hours for a chemical like caffeine to affect us? Yes, that is right, 48 hours! So if you wanted to be sure you were wide awake for an important meeting on Thursday morning, you would have to drink your coffee on Tuesday.

So why do ingested chemicals (like the caffeine in coffee) affect us so much faster, usually in 20 to 30 minutes? What is really happening is that when the chemical is digested and enters into the blood stream, it is like a miniature radio station, emitting a particular frequency. This is the characteristic frequency of the chemical; everything we ingest – foods, drugs, supplements, coffee, whatever – all has its own frequency that it broadcasts. This broadcast has an extremely short range, and the chemical needs to be carried through the bloodstream so that its broadcast can reach all the cells of the body.

The mechanism of a chemical triggering a cell's receptor for that chemical is often thought of as a lock and key mechanism, where the chemical is the "key" and has a specific shape that fits into the "lock" of the cell receptor. A more accurate analogy is that the chemical emits a frequency, like a tiny radio transmitter, and the cell receptor is like a radio receiver that responds when it senses that particular frequency. It is very much like the way that remote controls open car doors. When I approach my car and click the 'unlock' button, the remote generates a particular frequency that the car hears and responds to by unlocking the doors. Similarly, when caffeine enters the bloodstream, it broadcasts a frequency that the body's cells respond to, causing us to feel more alert and awake.

This may seem outlandish, but there have actually been experiments done that prove this. In one experiment, the frequency emitted by a particular antibiotic used to kill E-coli bacteria was isolated. Then frequency generators were used to create this frequency throughout the body, and it was found that the e-coli bacteria were killed just as effectively by using the frequency generators as by taking the antibiotic!

So, truly, science has shown us that we are simply big piles of complicated frequencies, and by introducing new frequencies into our systems our bodies and our lives will respond.

Those interested to learn more are encouraged to reference the book *The Field* by Lynne McTaggart, which discusses these scientific experiments and the concept of "everything is just frequency" in greater detail..

Other Healing and Manifestation Modalities

Within this framework, other modalities and all the Seven Planes are simply different ways of creating different frequencies. Crystals and rocks have their own frequencies and so now we can see how the proper combination of crystals and rocks (First Plane energies) can create exactly the right frequencies to heal any life problem, including illness, injury, poverty, loneliness, or depression. Anything!

Similarly, every plant and herb has its own frequency, so the proper combination of plants and herbs (Second Plane energies), truly can heal anything. The same goes for all of the planes. Everything is just frequency, so no matter how you generate those frequencies, applying the proper frequencies to the human body will result in shifts and changes in that person.

Our Lives as Cosmic Radio Tuners

When we turn on a radio, the radio has a tuner we can use to pick the frequency that the radio is receiving. So, I might set the tuner to 106.7 FM and as a result the radio might start playing rock music. If I do not like the rock music, I can tune it to 99.1 FM, which may be playing country music. If I do not like the country music, I can tune to a different frequency that is playing classical music or broadcasting a sporting event or a talk radio program. In essence, there are a large number of different signals being broadcast across the radio spectrum and we use our radio to tune into the exact signal we want to listen to.

Our lives work in much the same way. A powerful metaphor for understanding the experience of life on Earth is to think of the Universe as a radio station that broadcasts every type of signal, including all kinds of sound, talk, music, etc. The radio transmitter of the Universe does not just broadcast every type of signal imaginable, but **in fact it broadcasts every type of signal possible**, on infinite frequencies.

As human beings, the sum total of the frequencies of our being, as described through the four levels of the subconscious, causes us to "tune in" to one particular signal being broadcast by the Universe. This signal we then receive from the Universe is truly our "song of life"!

Much as we can use the radio tuner to listen to different music and radio programs, we can tune our internal frequencies to modify our "song of life", which is composed of our physical health, our relationships, and our level of prosperity — **everything!** Just as you can change the dial on your radio if you do not like the signal being broadcast by the station you are listening to, you can change your subconscious software codes so that you are tuning into a different signal being broadcast by the Universe on a different frequency.

Don't like the experience of being sick? Simply retune yourself to hear a different signal from the Universe, and experience health! Much as we can flick our wrist and instantly hear a different radio program, you can change your internal frequencies with Theta Healing and instantly tune into a new "song of life" without your sickness. Welcome to an instant miracle healing!

Understood in this context, instant miracle healings and amazing manifestations seem much more believable. All of our masters and self help gurus have been telling us the same thing for decades: to change what is outside of you, you must start by changing what is inside of you.

The radio metaphor fits perfectly here. If your radio is tuned to 98.7 FM, and you do not like the music, one thing you can do is go to the radio station and try to convince them to play different music. This is likely to take a lot of your time and energy, and most of the time you will fail and the radio station will continue to play the same old music that you do not like. Instead, it would be much easier for you to simply tune your radio dial to a different frequency to hear music that you prefer.

Most of us approach our lives by trying to change the things external to us, such as the size of our bank account, other people's behavior, etc. As with trying to get a particular radio station to play different music, this takes a lot of time and energy and usually does not work. A much easier and more effective approach is to simply change the codes in your subconscious software so that you are tuning into a different signal – a new "song of life" – being broadcast by the Universe.

It may seem too simple and too good to be true at first, but this is how the Universe works. If you want to change your life, in whatever form – eliminating health problems, manifesting wealth and abundance, experiencing joyful and loving relationships – the fastest and most effective way is to simply change the codes inside of yourself and tune into a different experience of life.

This makes even more sense when we again invoke the Parallel Worlds theory of quantum physics. When we understand the Multi-verse (meaning a collection of all the different Universes) as containing every possible different version of Universe, it becomes much easier to understand how instant healings and manifestations can take place.

For example, if you have a health problem in your current Universe, then there is some other Universe in the Multi-verse that is exactly like your current Universe, except that you are healthy. In order for you to heal and experience perfect health, you do not have to actually change anything outside of yourself; instead, you can adjust your internal subconscious software to tune into a slightly different signal, or song of life, effectively shifting you into a parallel Universe where you are healthy. Instant healing achieved!

Similarly, if you are poor in your current Universe, you do not actually have to change anything outside of yourself to become wealthy. Instead, you only need to adjust your internal subconscious software to tune into a slightly different signal, or song of life, where you are wealthy. Instant manifestation achieved!

Invoking parallel Universes may seem like a bizarre concept, but in fact the idea of multiple Universes has been accepted as real by much of the scientific community. Each time you make a decision in life, no matter how small, you are shifting into a slightly different Universe. For example, if you are considering having either a pizza or a hamburger for dinner, then there is one Universe in which you have the pizza, and another parallel Universe where you have the hamburger. This is the fundamental nature of reality, and when we understand this, it explains how instant healing and magical manifestations are indeed not only possible, but practical!

With a technique like Theta Healing, this process of changing your internal software to alter your song of life has been demystified and turned into a linear, understandable, precise, methodical approach that makes it really simple and easy.

There really is a *Formula for Miracles*, and we all carry it inside of ourselves. And given all the pain, suffering and other terrible experiences in the world on both the individual and societal levels, it is about time we started using it!

Metaphysical Engineering for Practical Miracles

I understand instant healings and manifestations and remote viewing and angel readings and all the other aspects of so-called psychic or paranormal phenomena as simply another form of engineering. To distinguish it from other types of engineering, I call this metaphysical engineering.

What is metaphysical engineering? In a nut shell, metaphysical engineering is the sum total of the techniques, algorithms, approaches and understandings we use to reprogram the subconscious software so that we are tuning into a different "song of life" that we prefer to our current life.

As an engineer myself, I like to emphasize the engineering aspect of healing. An engineer is just someone who is able to apply scientific understandings, observations and techniques to achieve a practical goal. By developing a deep understanding of the medium they are working in, engineers are able to achieve feats – such as building bridges or sending men to the Moon – that seem magical to others.

Is it necessary or even desirable to use an engineering approach to accomplish a task? Sometimes "no", and sometimes "yes", depending on your task. For example, say you want to build a dog house in your back yard. Do you need to hire architects and structural engineers for this task? Of course not; you can buy everything you need at the local hardware store, and with little or no training you can probably successfully build a dog house on a lazy Sunday afternoon.

By contrast, say you wish to build a skyscraper, like the Empire State Building. In this case, calling some friends and heading to the hardware store will likely not result in you building a successful skyscraper! Instead, your best chance at success is to work with people who are engineering experts in the appropriate fields. For a skyscraper, you need well-trained architects and structural engineers to design the building using precise, methodical techniques and the proper materials to ensure that the skyscraper will succeed and become a safe and structurally sound building. Because building a skyscraper is a much harder problem than building a dog house, it is imperative to use good engineers and the best techniques, methods, and materials possible to maximize the chance of creating a successful building. You could try to build a skyscraper the same way you build a dog house, but you are unlikely to be successful, and if you are not careful many people may be injured or die if the building collapses.

Engineers are trained in practical techniques to make things happen and achieve a specific result. Many people do not realize that the primary challenges of doing things like sending men to the Moon are not scientific challenges, but rather engineering challenges.

Of course, some engineering applications are destructive – like building weapons – but most are not, and nearly all of our modern-day conveniences are triumphs of engineering. Indoor plumbing, automobiles, air travel, and irrigation of otherwise uninhabitable deserts (such as the entire Los Angeles area) exist as a result of successful engineering. What engineers do is to take scientific understandings and apply them for practical purposes, using principles scientists have discovered.

Personally, I find that approaching healing work as metaphysical engineering yields excellent results. By applying the precise, methodical, controlled and linear techniques of engineering to healing and manifestation, it is possible to achieve powerful and immediate practical results.

Does it have to be done this way? Of course not! There are amazing healers in the world who know nothing of science or engineering techniques. I would not say that my method of metaphysical engineering is the best way for everyone, but both myself and my Theta Healing students have had incredible and consistent results by approaching healing and manifestation as metaphysical engineering.

Perhaps more importantly, large portions of our society – including many of our engineers, scientists, doctors, lawyers, business executives and others trained as analytical, linear thinkers – have felt alienated from the world of metaphysics, healings, miracles and psychic phenomena because they are not comfortable with the touchy-feely, "woo woo" nature of energy healing. The message of this book is that there is another approach – one that is linear, precise, methodical, consistent and practical – for creating a true *Formula for Miracles*™ that we can apply to our own lives.

Approaching instant healing and other metaphysical phenomena as software engineering on the subconscious mind is not the only way to achieve miracles, but it a great way for many people. We really can learn to create miracles in a way that appeals to the linear, analytical, skeptical nature of the modern Western mind.

It Only Works Because You Believe (Subconsciously) It Will

Now this is going to start getting really weird. Why is it that the approach of metaphysical engineering works so well, but yet people also achieve success with other more imprecise, fuzzy approaches? In a nut shell, things work or do not work for you in part *because* you (subconsciously) believe that they will or will not. More specifically, any technique or modality for healing or manifestation or whatever will work, if the codes in your subconscious software say that it will work for you. Conversely, no technique or modality – no matter how powerful or how talented or famous the practitioner – can work for you if the codes in your subconscious software say that it will not.

I have had powerful and consistent success with my metaphysical engineering approach to Theta Healing, not necessarily because it is inherently better than other approaches and styles, but because the codes in our modern, analytical minds tell us that the precise, methodical, linear, engineering approach to healing is effective. Commonly, many of us have codes within us that say that we cannot let things work for us until we understand them, so an easy way around this block to getting amazing results from healings is to use an approach that can be understood.

Is it possible to reprogram the subconscious software so that we are open to getting good results from other techniques and styles? Of course it is, but it may not always be easy or fast thing to do so. Personally, I always seek to bring the maximum healing and benefit to my clients and students in the shortest amount of time. So, when a client comes to me and wants to do a private Theta Healing session to work on their problems, the fastest way to bring them results is to work with them where they are at. For many of us living in the modern, technological Western world, we are more ready to accept and benefit from a technique that seems more precise and linear than from the "touchy-feely", "woo-woo" approach of many traditional psychics and healers.

One approach or style is not inherently better than another. However, particular people with particular problems may get results and heal much faster with one modality or style of healer than another. Personally, I have found people to be most receptive and get the most benefits from my "metaphysical engineering" approach to healing, because it always them to quickly and easily grasp how the healing will take actually occur. But things only work because we think they will; for people who have codes in their subconscious software that say that my approach (or any other) will not work for them, it may not!

Fate, Free Will, and the Meaning of Life

Now we have a much clearer understanding of how the Universe works, and in particular how we can use theta brainwaves and certain subconscious reprogramming techniques (such as Theta Healing) to fix the bugs in our internal software and create a new experience of life. But understanding "how" begs the question of "why?"

What does it mean that we are essentially powerful little creation computers, manifesting our body and our life experiences out of the codes within us?

What about our life purpose, or our soul's journey? How do these fit in?

Let us return to the online game metaphor, because I find it to be a remarkably accurate and insightful model of what life is really about. Earlier we explored the basics of how online games work, where each player has a computer that runs the game client software and connects over a computer network (the Internet) so that all the players can play together in the same game. The client software is full of codes that create the graphical depiction of the world, as well as all the sounds, architecture, artificial intelligence and the rules of the game. And by changing these codes, we can change our experiences in the game.

Our lives as humans on Earth are very similar. We all have computers (our bodies) and our game client software (our subconscious mind) and we are connected together via the cosmic Internet for our shared experience of life on Earth. If we do not like some aspect of our lives, we have the power within us to reprogram our internal software to create a different life experience. There are various ways to do this, but I have found the Theta Healing technique to be by a good margin the fastest, most powerful, and longest lasting technique.

Why do we play computer games? Quite simply, for the experience of it! We play games because they are fun and make us happy. Some people are highly completive and just play to win, but even that is still the same reason, since they play the games because they enjoy the experience of winning. There is really no other point to computer games; we just play them because we enjoy the experience.

Life is the same. Why do we come to Earth and live in human bodies in what can be an often difficult, frustrating and disappointing world full of suffering, wrong doing and hardship? Quite simply, we do it because our souls enjoy the experience. Being on the other side of the veil, as a being of pure energy that is one with everything, we can conceptualize and know about things such as passion, love, joy and good food, but we cannot experience them without descending into duality and living in a body.

It is the difference between reading a menu and looking at pictures of food, and actually tasting it. No matter how many pictures of and descriptions of pizza you look at, it cannot give you the same experience as actually eating a pizza. So that is why we come to Earth: for the experience of actually eating the pizza! (Who would have thought life was all about eating pizza?)

Life Purposes

Many of my clients and students are often concerned about their life's purpose. Others might call this their life's work or their soul's journey or doing God's work. Is this something we need to be concerned with?

The answer is a resounding **no**! Truly, the game of life is rigged. You cannot help but win, no matter how poorly you play -

because the object of the game is simply the game itself! To return to our computer game metaphor, after you play a computer game, you get up from the computer and return to your life, and whether or not you won the game is generally totally irrelevant to what comes next in your life (going to sleep, going to work, eating dinner, etc.) That is, except for the fact that you have been changed by the experience of the game.

But, just because the game of life is rigged so that you always win, does not necessarily mean you will enjoy the game. It is quite possible to play a game and find it a terrible experience, perhaps boring or even worse frustrating and painful, even if you win. Life is the same, except that you will win every time, guaranteed. However, the game may not always be 'fun'.

One metaphor that helps us understand this is seeing our life's journey as a road trip from Los Angeles to New York City. When you set out on this trip, you are guaranteed that you will reach your destination, since the trip has been rigged so that no matter what you do, you will sooner or later reach New York and be finished. This is the "big picture" of our lives, and it is largely created by the divine part of ourselves (the soul or higher self) that most of us are not consciously aware of. However, free will comes in when you determine the specifics of your journey, and most importantly, what you chose to make of the experience. It is entirely up to you and your free will to decide how we travel the road of life. You can choose to travel in a first-class carriage, with champagne and caviar and entertainment and massages and have a wonderful time. You can also choose to ride in a stinky bus that is breaking down every 5 miles. Or you might be driving in your own sports car, riding the highway at high speed as you crank your favorite tunes over the stereo. Or you might be walking beside the road, dragging a broken leg, sick and in pain and being chased by wild animals. (You could also be in this position, and have the wisdom and fortitude to be happy anyway, since attitude matters as much or more than circumstances.)

But, no matter how you choose to travel the road of life, you are guaranteed to end up at the proper destination at the end of your journey, as the game is rigged so you cannot fail.

Where you end up in life, and whether you accomplish your soul's journey, has been rigged so you cannot fail. It is simply impossible! No matter what you do, with every breath you take, with every move you make, you are accomplishing your life's mission. **You cannot fail in this!** But you can create an experience that is painful and difficult or one that is joyous and wonderful, and this is where free will comes in. And with a powerful technique of subconscious reprogramming such as Theta Healing, we have been given a profound tool to modify the details of our life's journey so that we can make it much more pleasant.

Life is like a *Choose Your Own Adventure* book, written by the divine part of you (the higher self or soul). And the book has been written so that, no matter what choices you make, and no matter what path you travel, you will always end up "winning" at the end of the story So, there are no "right" or "wrong" paths to take, except for what your belief systems tell you .

Every path through life is valid, and every path is guaranteed to accomplish your life's purpose, but you have the power of free will to decide exactly how it plays out and to choose how you experience it. Is it fun? Is it painful? Is it joyful? Is it a struggle? These are all options, and you can use your free will to choose among them. If you find yourself on a path that you do not like, just reprogram yourself to fix those bugs to put yourself on a different life path that you will enjoy more!

Finale

I hope that you have found this book empowering and informative. We really are gods walking the Earth, and with some reprogramming of our internal software we can tune into a completely different experience of life. Instant healings, amazing prosperity, supportive and loving relationships, and anything else we can imagine is finally within our grasp now that we have a technique like Theta Healing that lets us consciously create a life of our choosing.

Joy, love, health and prosperity are truly our birthrights, and we all have the power within us to heal or manifest anything, no matter how large, difficult or impossible our problems may seem.

THERE REALLY IS A FORMULA FOR MIRACLES!

Appendix A: The Formula for Miracles™ Technology

For the first several years that I was involved with Theta Healing, there were only two ways to apply it:

- Private sessions with professional practitioners
- Taking the Basic Theta Healing training seminar (described in Appendix C)

After I experienced the miraculous instant healing of my elbow in my first Theta Healing session in 2003, I made it my life's work and mission to master, share, teach, and expand upon Vianna's work.

And as a technologist, engineer, and visionary, I knew I had to find a way to help more than one person at a time!

The first step towards this goal was the introduction of my group healing events, starting with the *Wealth Club* in 2005, where I do healing on all participants to clear everyone's blocks to wealth and prosperity. I later added the *Love Club* tele-seminar, where I do group healing on love and relationship issues, and the *Health Club* tele-seminar, where I clear blocks to health, age reversal, and weight loss. These regularly scheduled group healing tele-seminars have become the foundation of my *Formula for Miracles VIP Club*, described in Appendix B.

The group healing tele-seminars are an easily affordable way to way to get powerful clearing of subconscious blocks, but I knew I could do better – my vision was to find a way to bottle the power of Theta Healing and encode it into audio programs such that people could get their subconscious blocks cleared just by listening to them!

After years of research and experimentation, I finally devised a way to charge the energy of Theta Healing into audio programs prepared with a special audio technology known as binaural beats. I call this the *Formula for Miracles*™ technology, and (as of the printing of the second edition of this book in 2010) it has been granted both patent-pending and trademark-pending status.

By combining applied kinesiology (aka muscle testing), sub-audible coding of binaural beats, and charged Theta Healing energy, these audio programs will actually put you into a deep theta brainwave and clear your subconscious blocks!

The great advantages of this technology are that:

- It is super simple and easy to use

- It is far less expensive than doing a similar amount of clearing in private sessions, and

- It does not require attending a live tele-seminar

The first product developed using this technology was *Unleash Your Inner Millionaire,* which focuses on wealth, prosperity, and success. The program includes material that lets you:

- **Clear the 327 most common blocks to prosperity and financial success**
- **Identify and clear the 6 greatest fears that hold**

you back from success
- **Learn the #1 mistake made that prevents the Law of the Attraction from working for you**
- **Learn the 12 most important things to always do when manifesting**
- **Learn the 16 most common mistakes that cause**

your manifestations to fail
- **Find what is blocking you from living "in the now"**

It includes approximately 8 hours of lecture and guided healing to clear subconscious blocks to wealth and unleash *your* inner millionaire!

I truly believe that the sky is the limit with this technology, as it allows for the energy of Theta Healing to be bottled into an audio program and made available to help people around the world.

At the time of the printing of the second edition of this book, the following products using the *Formula for Miracles*™ technology have either been released or are in development:

- *In Love for a Lifetime*, a comprehensive audio program (similar to *Unleash Your Inner Millionaire*) to clear blocks to having incredible love, romance, sex, and intimacy in your life.

- *Allergy Clearing Meditation*, which is a guided healing meditation designed to clear any kind of allergy that affects you.

- *The Spiritual Weight Loss Audio Program,* a comprehensive audio program (similar to *Unleash Your Inner Millionaire*) to clear blocks to weight loss, exercise, and a healthy relationship with food.

- *Trauma Clearing Meditation*, which is a guided healing meditation designed to clear the trauma, shock, and cellular trauma imprinted upon your subconscious by traumatic experiences, no matter whether the event occurred in your current life, happened to your ancestors, or affects you via a past life memory.

Of course, by the time you read this, there may be many more products and programs available to help you heal yourself quickly, automatically, and easily, anywhere and anytime!

Appendix B: The *Formula for Miracles* VIP Club

"*I had migraine headaches since I was a child...one session of Theta with Brent, and I've had no headaches for months!*"

"I have had migraine headaches since I was a child! I was taken to a number of doctors over the years who equated them with being triggered by food allergies, emotional issues, stress or possibly family history...and all of these things could absolutely trigger the most debilitating of headaches, many lasting for days at a time.

Over time I tried many different things to try to help make living with migraines more bearable, because once you have migraines , you're just prone to getting them...so you just learn to live with and adjust yourself for when they hit your world! In fact my migraines got so bad, one actually led to a bleed in my brain.

I recently learned about Theta Healing and Brent Phillips. I was very intrigued. I read Brent's book on Theta Healing, and was so impressed that I took his Theta weekend course to learn all I could. I loved learning about this very powerful tool which healed him instantaneously and learned how he came into this amazing information first hand!

I was becoming a student of Theta myself, but I had not actually had a healing done by Brent. And this was one of the most powerful and life changing experiences I have had!

One session of Theta with Brent and I've had no headaches for months, and before I would have on average one a week...and the difference is I don't expect to get migraines anymore, because during the session I literally felt something shift in my field and a big change occurred in my head as well my entire body! It was so completely noticeable.

Profound! Blessings to you on the highest!

NYEE M.
West Hollywood, California

I developed the *Formula for Miracles VIP Club* as a way to provide frequent updates and new material to my "Inner Circle" of those who are serious about transforming their lives. It is designed to give you a tremendous amount of value at a very low price so that everyone can take advantage of the power of Theta Healing.

In short, the VIP Club provides you with all the ongoing support, tools, and resources to let you continuously clear your subconscious blocks to the most important things that we all want in life: health, wealth, love, and happiness!

The *Formula for Miracles VIP Club* is a Web-based subscription service that offers a variety of frequently-updated resources to support your personal growth and spiritual development. These include:

- A monthly special event focusing on the "topic of the month", with custom created special videos, articles, forums, and daily exercises to help you move forward in your life.

- Access to all *Wealth Club* tele-seminars (plus recordings of all events in the last 90+ days)
- Access to all *Love Club* tele-seminars (plus recordings of all events in the last 90+ days)
- Access to all *Health Club* tele-seminars (plus recordings of all events in the last 90+ days)
- Discounts on private sessions
- Priority access to submit blocks to clear on the group healing tele-seminars
- Access to forums and private messaging where I will personally answer all of your questions
- Access to all question & answer sessions and tele-seminar special events (such as the *DNA, DNA Activation, and Epi-genetics* special call)
- Access to all online/tele-conference Theta Healing practice groups, where you can hone your skills (if you are a Theta Healing practitioner), or get a free healing from one of my students (if you are not a practitioner)
- Priority "beta" access to free versions of upcoming unreleased books, videos, classes, and audio programs
- Discounts on Theta Healing training seminars

It's super user friendly and easy to use, even if you know nothing about computers!

You'll receive a series of follow-up emails that show you how to use the different VIP Club resources, and you'll get access to a series of tutorial videos that show you step-by-step exactly how to log in and log out, how to cancel, how to download articles, how to access recorded tele-seminars, etc.

Some examples of previous special events are:

- "8 Days to Prosperity" (March 2010)
- "Spring into Health" (April 2010)
- "The Five Languages of Love" (May 2010)
- "Seven Simple Steps to Happiness" (June 2010)
- "Pain Begone!" (July 2010)

My goal with the VIP Club is to provide you with such an overwhelming amount of value that you'd be crazy not to at least give it a shot for 30 days to see how it can help transform YOUR life!

If you purchased this book either from my Web site *www.ThetaHealingLA.com* as part of a package, or through a third party such as via a tele-seminar special offer package, you should have received a 30 day membership in the *Formula for Miracles*™ *VIP Club* as part of your purchase – I hope to "see" you online soon!

Appendix C: Learning to Create Your Own Miracles

"I stand a smoke free and truly impressed man, who owes his life to Brent"

"I have been a smoker for almost 15 years... I was up to about 2.5 packs a day... I have not had a smoke since my session... I did not even have the associated headaches I usually got when I tried to go cold turkey.

As a business person, I am usually skeptical at anything I have either never heard of, or is too good to be true. Such was my experience with Theta Healing. I have been a smoker for almost 15 years it started innocently enough you know the usual he smokes so should I to be cool kinda thing. Well eventually I was dependent on them in fact I was up to about 2 and ½ packs a day so I hear about this fella who did this healing thing, I was like whatever, so being curious I decided to chat to this Brent fella and see just what this was about.

Can I say WOWZERs? I mean I went into my session set in stone that it was fake a hoax not possible all those thoughts but I will be damned I have not had a smoke since my session, and I find myself drinking more water now, I did not even have the associated headaches I usually got when I tried to go cold turkey.

I stand a smoke free and truly impressed man, who owes his life to Brent – I mean I was sick, addicted to things I knew were killing me yet I still smoked them, thankfully Brent and Theta saved me from the destructive path I was on and set me straight.

Thanks for the Help!

ANGELO S.
Medford, Massachusetts

It is the author's purpose and mission to promote and teach the technique of Theta Healing. It is a technique of creating ***practical, attainable miracles;*** Theta Healing provides ***instant healing with lasting results!***

From this site, you can contact Brent Phillips, view a list of upcoming Theta Healing events, including group healing classes (such as The Wealth Club), as well as upcoming Theta Healing training seminars.

Because Theta Healing techniques and self help seminars are generally applicable to so many areas of life, people of all sorts are drawn to the Theta Healing work.

- Some seek relief from chronic injury or illness.
- Some are natural intuitives who are seeking a refined technique to use their abilities more powerfully and more beneficially.
- Some seek to use Theta to build a business or manifest a compatible soul-mate.
- Some are spiritually focused and seek to connect more closely to the Creator of all that is.
- Some are fascinated with learning to do true magic in the real world.
- Others recognize that the world is going through some difficult, dark times and needs more light workers to help raise the vibration of the Earth and create a more enlightened civilization.

Whatever your interest, Brent and many others have found Theta Healing techniques to be the most powerful and profound tool available to us to shift and heal ourselves and those around us.

In the Basics of Theta Healing seminar, you will learn the following:

- The story of how Theta Healing began and how it has grown and evolved
- The brain waves and how they are important in the healing process
- About the 7 planes of existence
- How to cultivate a theta brainwave state and use it to connect directly to the creative Source
- How to muscle test yourself and other people to reveal subconscious beliefs
- How to draw on unlimited Source energy for readings and healings, instead of depleting your own energy
- How to do intuitive readings (looking inside the body)
- How to perform instant healings – locally and remotely, individually and in groups
- How to see and speak with guardian angels and guides
- How to do remote viewings and future readings
- How to change your DNA, including activating your youth and vitality DNA
- How to test and change subconscious beliefs on the 4 different levels (core, genetic, history, and soul)
- How to find the subconscious core beliefs underlying an illness, injury, or other challenge
- How to apply the Theta technique to improve your and others' physical health, mental attitude, and overall well-being

- How to work with the Universe to co-create your life exactly the way YOU want it to be

After completing the Basics of Theta Healing seminar, you will be registered with Nature's Path (Vianna Stibal's company) as a certified Theta Healing practitioner. This qualifies you to take the Advanced Theta Healing class from any certified instructor. The Advanced Theta Healing class is amazing and a lot of fun, and includes the following topics and more:

- How to see and speak with your deceased ancestors
- How to change hundreds of thousands of subconscious belief systems all at once with downloads
- How to clear free floating memories (also known as Engram Banks) out of the subconscious from surgery, abuse, war, or other trauma
- How to use Theta Healing on inanimate objects such as your home or car
- How to use Theta Healing on plants
- How to heal broken hearts
- How to heal broken souls
- How to bend time (yes, really – you can use Theta Healing to bend time and make it seem to go faster or slow – both awesomely cool and extremely useful!)

For more information, or to register for a private session or an upcoming seminar, please visit _www.Theta HealingLA.com_

Appendix D: *Secrets of Muscle Testing* Companion DVD

"I just finished watching your Secrets of Muscle Testing DVD. It's just tremendous! I have already sent your website to several of my acquaintances who are in need of some real healing in their lives with the recommendation that they go to your site and order the DVD. Just amazing how clearly you explained it all--it's almost as good as having you in the room!"

DR. TED T.
Palm Springs, California

- -

Theta Healing LA has leveraged its years of experience with Theta Healing and muscle testing to produce a DVD video specifically designed to teach you a wide range of muscle testing secrets, so you can muscle test yourself and others, quickly and easily.

The *Secrets of Muscle Testing* DVD is the companion DVD to this book, and provides live, visual demonstrations of all the muscle testing processes and procedures described in this book, as well as additional muscle testing tricks and tips not presented here.

Whether you are brand new to muscle testing, or an experienced Theta Healing or other holistic therapy

practitioner, this DVD is a treasure trove of tips, tricks, and troubleshooting techniques that will let you easily muscle test anyone.

What is on the DVD?

The DVD begins with an overview and explanation of muscle testing, explaining how we can use muscle testing to test the

subtle electrical and magnetic field around our body and see what is in our own subconscious mind.

Next, the DVD presents detailed, visual explanations of performing four different types of muscle testing:

- The Standing Method
- The Finger Ring Method
- The Arm Lever Method
- The Pendulum Method

The DVD covers both self-testing (where you can muscle test yourself without needing a partner) and partner testing (where you work with another person to muscle test.)

The last section is devoted to troubleshooting, explaining many different tricks, tips, techniques, and processes that can be used to help everyone get clear muscle testing results.

Even if you already are familiar with these methods of muscle testing, the DVD will offer many refinements and subtle adjustments that you can make to provide clearer, more accurate, faster muscle testing, even with people who normally have a lot of trouble muscle testing.

Do I need to know how to do Theta Healing to use this DVD?

No! The DVD is designed so that **anyone** can **quickly** learn how to do muscle testing!

Do I need this DVD if I have taken the Basics of Theta Healing seminar?

Yes! While muscle testing is covered in the Basics of Theta Healing seminar, this DVD goes into a level of detail with muscle testing that is beyond the knowledge and experience of most Theta Healing instructors. So even if you have been doing Theta Healing for years, you'll still be able to pick up new tips and tricks about muscle testing from this DVD.

Many Theta Healing practitioners are uncomfortable with muscle testing simply because they have not been given the proper training to do it correctly, accurately, and easily. As a result, it is quite unfortunate that many practitioners either minimize or completely avoid using muscle testing, which is a great disservice to both themselves and their clients.

How do I get mine?

You can get the Secrets of Muscle Testing DVD at *www.ThetaHealingLA.com*

Appendix E: *Deep Theta Meditation* Companion CD

"I purchased your CD about a month ago and it has been invaluable. To meet a deadline, my husband was working all hours of the day with very little sleep. However, he found that using the 45 minute meditation a couple of times during the day was sufficient to refresh and recharge him, both mentally and physically. I routinely suffer from jet lag when we travel, but on a recent trip to the East Coast, I diligently used the 45 minute meditation prior to going to going to bed and found that the jet lag did not affect me. Thank you!" -

MEENAL K.
Camarillo, California

- -

Theta Healing LA and The Meditation Podcast _have joined forces to produce a meditation CD specifically designed to bring you to a deep theta brainwave to improve and enhance relaxation, healing, manifesting, and well-being.

The CD uses a proven technology known as "binaural beats", which are sub-audible beats that guide the brain into a deep meditative state. These binaural beats are combined with relaxing nature sounds, and require that you listen to the CD with headphones.

How do I use the CD?

Theta Healing LA and The Meditation Podcast Present

Binaural Theta Meditation

Vol. 1, "Well-being"

Used with headphones, the tones on this CD can lead to deep states of meditation, healing, relaxation, and well-being, by enhancing the powerful Theta brainwaves.

Because of the use of the binaural beat technology, all you need to do is listen to it with headphones on, close your eyes, and relax - and the CD will automatically take you into a deep theta brainwave.

Will this CD help my Meditation and Manifesting?

The CD is specifically designed to bring you to a deep theta brainwave, which is the brainwave associated with the most powerful meditations, healings, and manifestations.

There are many proven benefits to accessing a theta brainwave, including deep relaxation, improved sleep, pain relief, and balancing the hormones in the body. In particular, studies have shown that accessing a theta brainwave lowers the level of stress hormones in the body.

How do I get mine?

You can get the CD at *www.ThetaHealingLA.com*